A KISS BEHIND THE CASTANETS

My Love Affair with Spain

JEAN ROBERTS

To my dear friend Elaine

With much love

Jean Roberts.

x

For my family, with my love.
I owe you everything.

A Dream Fulfilled

I have always wanted a house in Spain. I have no real idea why I chose Spain but that was where it was always to be. I think I'd already started to fall in love with the country many, many years before I'd even visited. I loved Spanish art, from the passionate and colourful works of Velázquez to the equally passionate but somewhat bizarre and glorious works of Dalí. I found it fascinating and I wanted to know what kind of country could stir that fire. I loved the sound of a Spanish guitar and I wanted to see the passionate and vibrantly coloured flamenco.

In the 1960s, foreign travel was becoming more accessible to the masses; the package holiday was born. My friends were coming home from Lloret and Tossa with flamenco dolls; the dresses, poses, and vividly painted faces as fiery and impassioned as the paintings. I didn't want to own a doll. I wanted to feel the passion. I wanted to watch the dancers. I wanted to see, touch, and feel Spain. I wanted the country. The seeds of love had already been sown. A two-week holiday was never going to be enough; I wanted to live there.

My father had been a Far East Prisoner of War. He'd left

Glasgow during the Depression and joined the Royal Artillery, an old and fine regiment in the British Army. This took him far away to the exotic and exciting Far East. The horrors and deprivation of time spent under the brutal Japanese were completely taboo subjects but he would talk happily of the wonderful times he had out there before the fall of Singapore. I grew up with stories of Malaya and Singapore that filled me with enchantment and made my feet itch. They also filled me with a wanderlust that, thankfully, has never left me. His stories transported me across the globe. I wanted to see the world. The possibility of travel for me in those days was non-existent but one day I was going to go where he'd been and see what he'd seen. In the austerity of post-war Britain, in our council prefab, I listened to tales of rubber plantations, estates, and palaces. My dad knew the Sultan of Johor. Imagine!

I did, many years later, travel to the Far East on a heartbreaking journey to track his time as a prisoner there. I fulfilled my lifelong dream of seeing other lands and cultures. The dust of Europe is on the soles of my shoes; America, north and south, has been ticked off the bucket list; the South Seas, Panama, the pyramids of Egypt, all have taken a little bit of my soul but the pull for Spain was always there. A country I knew little about — apart from the odd short holiday here and there to Majorca or Menorca — but, if I was ever going to settle anywhere apart from England, that was where it was going to be.

As our two children were growing up, I would collect brochures from development companies in Spain and go to property exhibitions; the latest edition of *Homes Overseas* was my constant companion. As I got older and work became more and more stressful, the house in Spain became my escape route. I'd worked hard for my professional qualification and my position as a social work team manager and I prided myself on the standards of service we were providing. However, as time went on, workloads increased, budgets were restricted, and I found myself managing two teams until the situation became untenable. I was working from eight in the morning until midnight sometimes and, as duty manager, albeit for daytime only, people felt able to call me 24 hours a day.

In the days before answerphone and caller display, even on my wedding day, I logged up five hours on the telephone. There was no respite. Added to this, I was managing child protection with a team of largely unqualified workers, with an incompetent line manager who'd begun a relationship with the manager of the team we were meant to pass our cases to after we'd completed the initial assessment. Could I pass anything on? Could I heck! Pillow talk was winning out every day. The team was constipated. There was no stemming the flow coming through the front door daily and there was no release at the other end. We were all suffering. Trying to maintain a safe service to clients was unbelievably hard.

I should have walked away. I didn't.

I came into social work to make a difference but, with no management support, I spent my days firefighting and there was no way I could sustain that indefinitely. The service users were barely getting what they needed and I was going under.

On days when I was feeling completely overwhelmed, I would take ten minutes out to work on my three-year plan. I was getting to an age when I could realistically think about slowing down, taking early retirement, so I would sit for a few minutes and work out how this could be achieved. Plan, daydream, phone for another brochure; anything to gain a little bit of respite from the unrelenting pressure. It didn't matter if it failed to materialise; the dream made life bearable. Three years felt do-able. A short time-span, at the end of which I would be rich enough to retire and I would

Taking Ownership

Within a fortnight, I was on a plane to Malaga with John and his wife, Shirley, clutching a list of phone numbers and properties to be viewed, all under €30,000.

There were so many houses to choose from; some fairly squalid, some perfectly liveable, and so many, because of Spanish inheritance laws, abandoned and complicated. The price restriction took us inland to where property was cheaper and you got a lot more for the money. Despite this, because of our relatively small budget, all of the properties needed some form of renovation. Some needed a minor touch-up and modernisation and others a total rebuild. We went into some that kept animals inside; we stepped over obstacles and dog poo; in another the ceiling collapsed on us and we viewed one where the entire inside was missing. But we saw some charmers. Pretty, whitewashed villages where oranges grew in the streets, lovely village squares where families came to walk at night, and beautiful, breathtaking scenery. We achieved a lot that weekend.

One agent, Simon, gave us a lot of his time, took us to view several houses, and gave us a tour of the local area. We initially chose a house in a picturesque cobbled street; small, with only two bedrooms but with a huge roof terrace. There'd been others we'd liked but this was the only one with outside space.

We headed back to the office with Simon, paid our deposit, and signed the contracts. His partner, Alyssa, telephoned the owner who said she wanted to see us so off we trekked back to the house, only to find her son passed out, drunk, on the sofa. He wasn't happy that mama was selling his party house and so he'd decided to squat.

I left Alyssa arguing it out with the owner but rejoined her quickly to get away from John and Shirley who were arguing away on the roof. The upshot of this was that the owner was taking the house off the market and would re-think it in six months, perhaps when her son had sobered up.

'Back to the drawing board,' I sighed as we took another look at our options.

We'd seen another house we'd liked a lot, more than this one in fact, but we'd discounted it because of the lack of outside space. Attached to a church, the house only had a tiny patio, about the size of our dining table. The other problem was that it was with another agent. We'd planned to see a second estate agent that weekend but, in the end, we saw only Simon. He'd given us such good service that we were a little delayed for our appointment with the other agent. I telephoned to say we would be another ten to fifteen minutes and would he kindly wait. The response?

'Too bloody late! I'm halfway to Malaga now. I've got a pool and a round of golf waiting for me. I haven't got time to hang around for you buggers.'

Salesman of the year, without a doubt. I was too stunned to make a response.

We decided to stay with Simon and Alyssa who were able to secure the house from the other agent and we handed everything over to them. They'd been superb and had earned the sale. We'd chosen a townhouse in the lovely old town of El Nacarino (which means mother of pearl) that was sound and solid. It needed reforming but it had three bedrooms, a functioning toilet, and a nice feel to it. Basic, but it could have been lived in. Any changes would be down to us and what we wanted to do.

And now, having been back in the UK waiting for the necessary paperwork to be drawn up, we were on our way to Stansted to complete the purchase. Just another couple of hours and we would be walking out into sunshine.

The early morning drive to Stansted was cold, grey, and wet. The 6 a.m. departure meant leaving home at 3 a.m. to leave enough time to check in, clear security, and get to the gate in time to get a decent seat. It was too early for sunlight but, when daybreak came, it was still raining and dismal; just a different shade of grey. I thought about Adrian at home, still tucked up in our cosy warm bed, and wished he was coming with us. John and Shirley were OK but they wouldn't be my travelling companions of choice. Adrian had shown little interest in the house, certainly not enough to make the journey with us. He had some awful memories of food poisoning in Spain and was putting off visiting the country for as long as possible. Besides, as he reminded me, someone had to work to pay for this little adventure. He would come over later.

Buying a house in Spain should be an easy process. I'd read and researched enough to be aware of the risks to look out for. There were some real horror stories out there. What should be an exciting time has often been a dreadful experience for so many people. We were determined to avoid the pitfalls so we didn't become another statistic on the casualty list.

In our case we were lucky; we didn't experience any of the purchasing nightmares I'd read about. We paid our deposit and handed everything over to the solicitor recommended by our estate agent. From then on everything went smoothly. We gave the solicitor power of attorney to act on our behalf and heard no more until we needed to go over and sign to complete. We handed over a small amount of 'black' money in the notary's office (a practice now outlawed but common at the time) and the rest went through without a hitch, everything legal and pain-free.

Outside the notary's office, the solicitor gave us her bill, a handwritten piece of paper with two amounts on. The first, a higher charge if we wanted to pay tax, and the second, a much lower amount if we didn't as she would simply take the cash then and there. No wonder the Spanish economy was in so much trouble when even solicitors gave lessons in tax avoidance.

We walked back to the house in the sunshine.

'Cakes! You wanna cake, John?' Shirley suggested as we walked past a cake shop.

'Not for me, thanks.' Not that she'd even bothered to consider me. I shrugged. 'I've not got a sweet tooth. They do look delicious though. Adrian will love this place. What a bonus having it nearby.'

'Couldn't agree more,' mumbled John through a mouthful of flaky pastry.

In the narrow street outside the house, the three of us stood and looked. This was the first time we'd seen the place since the initial viewing. It was minuscule; the frontage was just a door, a window, and another minute window on the upper floor.

'Small, innit?' said John.

'Ohhh,' Shirley agreed.

I felt a little nervous. Each of us had memorised a much bigger house. It was too late now; we were standing there with the keys and title deeds. It was ours.

'Best go in then,' I suggested.

John unlocked the door and we walked in; proud, happy, but hesitant new owners of our first house in Spain. As the door opened, light flooded in and it was like a Tardis. It was huge! Our memories hadn't betrayed us. From the front window, the right wall went out at an angle, making the house wedge-shaped, the narrowest part of the wedge being at the front.

'There's a lot of work to be done,' I said. 'Uneven concrete floors, plaster blown on the walls... But it's beautiful!' I couldn't help smiling from ear to ear. Even in this state, the house was light and airy. It had potential. This was going to be OK.

John and Shirley

Adrian and John had become acquainted when he joined an off-roading club shortly after he bought a Wrangler jeep. After working all week, he liked nothing better than to get out onto some muddy tracks, slip and slide over hills and dunes, and generally create a load of laundry. He would come home soaking wet, caked in mud, and grinning from ear to ear. It was here he met John who was always there, covered in grime from previous weeks, with a foreign jeep held together with tape, wire, and all sorts of odds and ends. Anything that fell off or broke was immediately mended on site and, however battered his vehicle looked, it was clear a lot of love had gone into it. John was rough and ready, not so much a rough diamond, more uncut zircon, but his heart was in the right place.

John took a shine to Adrian and always sought him out. His bizarre and eccentric behaviour had caused him some problems at work apparently but generally he was OK with Adrian. When he'd suggested buying a house in Spain where they could take their jeeps, Adrian had been hesitant.

'We could get a fixer-upper, Ade. We could do that, no

in the middle of the name made a big difference. Shirley was having none of it.

'But if you think about it, it must be the right place. They wouldn't have two towns sounding the same. Think about it; it's got to be, innit? Stop someone and ask where the hotel is.'

Oh Lord, we had nearly another hour of this before we got to the hotel. Her inane chatter was bouncing off the inside of the small car. Nerves jangling by now, my hands gripped the steering wheel as if I were, at the same time, holding onto my sanity, my knuckles white as snow. A few minutes later, we had Shirley's final word on the subject before she slumped back in her seat and, thankfully, remained quiet for the rest of the journey.

'Well, oh, but, oh, that's daft, innit?'

Ordering dinner was like an afternoon in a nursery. John was a corpse-and-two-veg type of guy so his order of steak and chips was easy. Shirley, on the other hand, wanted paella, which the menu clearly stated was for two people. Trying to explain this was like swimming through treacle.

'But I only want one portion. I couldn't eat two.'

'You're not expected to eat two, Shirley. You need to choose something else; they don't do single servings.'

'But I want paella.'

'They'll only serve for two. It's not worth their while doing single portions.'

'How do you know that?'

'It says it on the menu.'

'Where? Oh... but... oh... well, I only want one.'

'Find something else, Shirley; there're lots of nice things to choose from.'

'John, she says I can't have paella,' she wailed, tears beginning to well.

'Shut up, yer daft cow.'

Not for the first time that day, I was subjected to a barrage of belches, burps, and farts as John's complete lack of social skills was put on display. In the very nice hotel restaurant, several heads turned as John opened his mouth wide to let the thunderstorm that was going on in his belly erupt in a loud, vibrating, rolling crescendo. Several times this rumble escaped and rattled around the restaurant. In between outbursts, he chomped away, mouth open wide at every chew, speaking and spraying as he ate, bits of food getting caught in his beard.

Several gut-churning belches later, I pushed my meal aside. I couldn't stomach any more.

'John, it's like eating with Fungus the Bogeyman.'

'Better out than in, eh, John?' trilled the delightful, but slightly brain-dead, Shirley, more of a statement than a question.

'No! No, it's not.'

Parp. *OMG! Did he just do what I think he did? Oh please, save me!*

Just at that moment, a Spanish family arrived and asked why we weren't in the next room with everyone else celebrating Holy Week.

'Come, come and join us.'

I was thankful John and Shirley didn't speak Spanish. At that moment I wished I didn't either. To my shame I didn't pass on the invitation, just pretended I hadn't understood.

John's uncouth behaviour went on all weekend. With complete disregard for where we were or whom we were with, John's belly rumble was vented. In the estate agent's office, I refused a drink, hoping John and Shirley would follow suit. No chance.

Negotiations over, we decided to buy two beds the same. The cheap ones. Then it was time to pay.

'John won't pay until they're delivered; he never does,' Shirley offered.

What? 'Shirley, we have to pay now or we won't get them.'

'But how do we know they'll be alright? What if we don't like them?'

'That's not how it works. We've chosen them and now we have to pay or we leave without buying; it's that simple.'

'Well, can you ask? Tell them we'll pay when we get them.'

'No.'

'Oh, but... oh...'

There was no way I was going to continue sleeping on a cement floor in our new house just so they could haggle over payment and, having made it clear I was *not* sharing a bed with John, illicitly or otherwise, I made to pay. John and Shirley very meekly did the same.

Perhaps I should've known how things were going to be with John. On that very first house-buying weekend, after we'd paid the deposit and were on our way to the airport in high spirits, John was chuckling and obviously very pleased with himself. 'We just bought a 'ouse,' he'd said and, to emphasise his extensive range of talents, he'd let out a simultaneous belch and fart, something that, right up until that moment, I'd thought was a special gift given only to goats.

Dodgy Builders

'Are there any overhead cables down your street?' The removal men asked me when they arrived at our house in England, ready to take some of our furniture to Spain amidst the renovation activity.

'No, there aren't,' I blithely answered. I genuinely believed that to be true. I was more concerned the men had come with a massive pantechnicon that hadn't a hope of negotiating the narrow winding streets of El Nacarino. Our small amount of furniture was loaded into a corner of this vast truck and it set off. When we arrived in Spain two weeks later, it was all safely stored in our living room. How it got there, I can barely imagine. It can't have been easy especially as, in addition to the narrowness of the streets, our road was festooned with overhanging cables for its entire length; by far the worst was the one that sagged horribly right outside our front door.

John and Shirley weren't interested in coming over yet. 'Me an' Shirley will go over for a holiday,' John told me, 'once all ve work's done.'

My friend Kim came over with me and we'd planned to

spend a few days out and about exploring the local area, eating delicious Mediterranean food, and sampling the local wines. I was going to do a little bit of work on the house and then we were going to have some fun. Kim was meant to relax.

For the next week, Kim and I worked solidly and into the small hours, opening boxes and assembling flat-pack furniture. What hadn't seemed a lot to look at turned out to be a huge amount of work as we put together sideboards, tables and chairs, bedside cabinets, CD racks, and chests of drawers to fill the living room, dining room, and three bedrooms. It was a week of ripping open boxes, hammering and drilling, screwing and assembling, lifting and carrying. Kim worked tirelessly and with good humour to help get everything done.

'I couldn't let you struggle on your own,' she said, possibly through gritted teeth. I couldn't tell because of the screws held in her mouth while her hands were full.

It was hardly the week in the sun she'd envisaged but she didn't complain and, if she had any evil thoughts, she kept them to herself. I don't know what I would have done without her; she was a Godsend.

At the end of the week, we were tired and blistered but I had a cosy, comfortable, fully furnished home and a pile of empty boxes that needed to be disposed of. Endless cups of coffee and bottles of wine were consumed as we cut, tore, stomped on, and folded a mountain of cardboard to be carried away by the midnight bin men. To this day Kim still blanches at the sight of a cardboard box. Surprisingly she hasn't bitten at any requests to come away with me again...

Under normal circumstances, if a builder says he can start

'this afternoon', any sensible person would make their excuses and leave. In our case, we met Tony and Sharon, a young couple, in the notary's office on the day we were completing our purchase. They were doing the same and completing on their house in the next village. They seemed nice; they were friendly and we knew no one. Tony told us he had years of experience in barn restoration in the UK and was planning to set up in business in Spain. He was just starting out and had no work so it would help us both. This young family would have an income and we would have renovations done in a language where communication would be no problem. It seemed an ideal situation. Perfect! Except it wasn't.

We had just a little time to look around our new house before Tony was to arrive. The upstairs was in almost perfect condition; it was only the downstairs that needed reforming. Even in its current state, it was habitable.

One of the pitfalls of buying a property abroad is not knowing what there is to know and not knowing the right people until *after* you've moved in i.e. the ones who knew the previous occupants, the ones who could tell you which builders to avoid like the plague, and the ones who could tell you that the nice lady you'll eventually entrust your keys to is the biggest crook in the area. No amount of prior research is going to tell you that.

We fell foul of the builder and the key holder.

Looking back I find it hard to believe how naïve and trusting I was in those days. All I can say in my defence is my work situation had weakened me and left me wanting to shy away from difficult situations. The old me would have tackled issues head on and dealt with them and not have been taken in so easily. My biggest mistake, sadly, was in trusting my fellow countrymen.

Soon the renovations were underway in El Nacarino and continued to be 'underway' for almost two years. Every time we questioned the slowness of progress, we received the explanation that it was a major job, it was going to take time, and it was 'a work in progress' that would develop. Because we had nowhere comfortable to stay, our time in El Nacarino had been limited to short bursts and we'd had no chance to meet anyone else or explore other options. It was also difficult to get anyone in to complete someone else's work. Another builder did come and have a look around, threw his hands up in despair, and left, muttering something about 'English houses' on his way out. We were in a hole so we stuck with Tony. Surely we would climb out of this pit soon; there really wasn't that much to do.

Better the devil you know? Don't you believe it.

I like to think we were simply trusting. I'm trying so hard not to use the words gullible and stupid but they're hard to get away from. We can't blame anyone else; we allowed ourselves to be taken advantage of. What do they say? If I knew then what I know now... Well, we didn't and we suffered for it.

One of the pitfalls of owning a house in one country and living in another is there has to be a lot of trust involved. It's very difficult to keep your eye on someone when you're a thousand miles away. We relied on Tony feeding us information and keeping us up to date with progress. Not the first, or only, mistake we were to make.

To move things along, my daughter Suzanne and I would come over for a week at a time and set to, knocking off blown plaster and scraping the walls. We worked hard and, at the end of a week, we could see what we'd done. The problem was we couldn't see what Tony had done, only that money was rapidly draining from our account.

There was a complete disregard for us and our personal property. We didn't have much there at the time, just some basic items that made life a bit more comfortable when we visited, but they were ours and we needed them. Our granddaughter, Eva, was still a baby and so we'd bought her an oversized washing up bowl to be used as a bath. We bought another, smaller, orange-coloured bowl for washing up.

One day Sharon, Tony's wife, said, 'I noticed you didn't have a washing up bowl so I've bought you one.'

'We don't need one,' I replied. 'We already have two.'

'No, there definitely isn't one in your house. I'll just add the two euros onto your bill.'

We later found Eva's bath discarded on a pile of rubble, full of solid cement from when her husband had used it. We never did find the orange one.

Our cutlery disappeared from the drawer and we found it used, heavy with concrete, and broken and, every time we came over, the gas bottles used for cooking needed replacing. As we were only over for five days at a time, it was obvious they were being swapped with empties from Tony and Sharon's own home but it was difficult to prove. The explanation given to us was we'd used them for the shower and so had 'gobbled up the gas'. I now know from experience that using a gas bottle for hot water, for a whole family, will last for two months or more. I doubted the explanation but, at the time, had no option but to accept it.

According to our bills, we'd bought enough tiles to seemingly furnish two houses. When I queried this, they told me there'd only just been the right amount; that they'd bought seconds to save us money and some needed to be discarded; there were breakages, etc, etc. In fact they needed to buy more. Short of counting every tile when it was laid, and it almost came to that, there was no way I could disprove Tony's claims they'd been used. There was also no way our tiny house could have accommodated the amount of bulk he claimed to be putting into it.

There was a carriage lamp put on an outside wall. He

positioned it so badly that, every time a door opened, it banged onto it. We asked Tony to move it. He did. He moved it to his own house and we never saw it again. He replaced it with a cheap, bulkhead light we already owned.

On one occasion we notified Tony and Sharon we would be coming to stay and we expected to see some progress.

'It looks lovely,' Sharon wittered. 'You'll be surprised. Tony has left it perfect for you. There's still some way to go but it will be good for you coming over.'

I arrived with Suzanne, Eva, and Findley, my daughter Chrystal's youngest son, to find the floor only half tiled, a pile of sharp sand in the middle of it, no doors, broken glass shattered everywhere, a cement mixer in the living room, and a pile of rubble pushed under the stairs. Perfect it was not, particularly as Eva was still crawling. It was a building site. Hardly what we'd expected or had been led to believe.

We moved everything upstairs to where it was clean and the children would be safer. We made a living room and two bedrooms and only came downstairs to use the kitchen and bathroom. How on earth could it take so long to reform just the lower half of this tiny house? It just didn't make sense. When we questioned Tony, he said it was just too much work for one person to do single handed and asked if he could take on a Spanish labourer. To move it along, we agreed.

The work did pick up the pace but it also became very expensive as we were paying for Tony and the labourer. The floors were tiled quickly and the cement mixer moved out but the place still wasn't ready. In hindsight we believe that, despite paying double wages, only the labourer had been working, especially as he turned up one day looking for payment and said he hadn't seen Tony all week. Tony responded that I'd misunderstood. 'Still having problems with the language, are we?'

Unattached electric cables stuck out of every wall and the

walls were still not plastered. He'd taken three months to channel them out for electricity. Did he use a router? Probably. An afternoon's work at most but he charged for several weeks. He then, supposedly, employed a Spanish electrician to come in and rewire. Definitely the wiring was there but it wasn't attached to anything. There were no plugs or switches.

But, finally, it was done! The walls were plastered; the floors were tiled; the new patio was laid and we had a usable bathroom. However, the wooden worktop we'd bought from IKEA for the kitchen, which looked fabulous when new, soon started to throw up problems as it hadn't been oiled or treated. We arrived one day to find the sink was drifting and the worktop was peaking at the corners. There were several inches of air between the top of the cabinets and the worktops. I called Tony.

'Well, you bought cheap IKEA,' he said. 'This is what happens. You should have bought granite.'

IKEA would be pleased.

There was nothing wrong with the worktop, just the neglectful and amateurish way it had been installed and prepared. It was completely unusable and needed replacing. This time we did use granite and we had someone else install it.

The new patio also caused us a major problem. The houses in El Nacarino were built into the side of a hill and so the neighbour's house was below ours. Tony had drained the patio straight into our neighbour's vestibule. No proper outlet, just a fancy hole that, every time it rained or I washed the floor, flooded out our neighbour.

Completely unaware it wasn't attached to the main drainage system, I was pouring buckets of dirty water into the drain and, horrifyingly, our neighbour was being deluged with our filthy dregs. The first time I became aware there was a problem, I'd just finished washing the patio and tipped the used water down the drain, just as I'd done each time before. Suddenly there was an anguished cry of, '¡AGUA!' from down below followed by a lot of indecipherable, angry Spanish. I may not have been able to understand it at the time but no words were needed to hear panic.

A short while later, a head popped around the open front door and called for me. My anxious neighbour from below wanted me to go with her to see the damage.

I went with her into her immaculate house, through into her pristine vestibule, passing her very grumpy husband on the way. My shamefaced 'hola' — hello — was met with a grunt. They obviously took pride in their home. Their pretty vestibule, festooned with decorative plates and flowers, was saturated. About halfway up the wall that adjoined our house, there was a drainage pipe sticking out, over which she'd placed a small metal basket, similar to the type used on the back of doors for collecting mail, only this time there was no mail. When she took it off, out tumbled a few very dead, very wet birds that had either scuttled in or been washed down the open drainpipe from our patio.

This was more than just a rain run-off. Tony had put a drainpipe directly from our patio into theirs. Everything — rain, dirty water, dust, dead animals — had been pouring into their lovely home. Poor people, no wonder they were upset.

While I was talking with the neighbour, their small, yappy, very excitable dog was bouncing around. To return the favour, in his excitement he peed on my foot.

Tony had also put an air brick into the external kitchen/patio wall without considering its correct location. Each time it rained — and it rains hard in Spain — water gushed into my kitchen and under the units. It also poured in through the front and back doors as he'd slanted the steps inwards, funnelling the water as it hit the doors straight into the house.

The new electric wiring looked very neat and worked a treat until we wanted to use three appliances at the same time. With the fridge permanently on, we were left with only one other appliance to use before we had a total blackout. It was impossible to have the kettle and the oven on at the same time and heaven help us if we needed a light on in more than one room at night as they overloaded the system. In the end we paid Endesa, the Spanish national electricity company, to upgrade the power and to secure the trailing cables that had been left drooping dangerously outside the house. Not only dangerous but unsightly, shoddy, and expensive to boot.

We'd had Tony cut stairs down into the kitchen. At first glance they were lovely; a really nice job. On using, they were awful, each step at a different height. One particularly bad one jarred the spine when it was forgotten.

The roof leaked in the bathroom and there were cracked tiles. We should have called Tony back in to correct all of this but I really couldn't be bothered. By this time I was sick to death of him and there was no way I would have him in my house again. There hadn't been a single job he'd tackled that had gone smoothly or parts of which didn't need re-doing.

I finally tired of hearing how Tony had used his 'nous' to get things done and how he'd done us big favours with special things he was helping us with. He used his 'nous' alright and fleeced us out of a small fortune. Fifty thousand euros, to be precise.

In the end we employed Paco, a Spanish builder, which is what we should have done in the first place, to put everything right.

We later heard from other expats who were similarly ripped off by Tony. On one occasion he was caught charging for work he wasn't doing and for materials he'd bought for his own house. On another, the owner turned up unexpectedly for the day. Tony put in a bill for seven hours supposedly worked on that day. He was robbing people blind while at the same time spinning fantasies about the work he was doing and how wonderfully the renovations were taking shape.

His reputation in El Nacarino was badly tarnished but, undoubtedly, he will have moved on to some other gullible expat and will have his hands in their pockets, 'using his nous'. Reputations, like bad odours, tend to hang around for a while and, if not dealt with, foul other areas. I don't doubt that the reputation of other Brits in the area has been tainted by this particular cowboy's lack of integrity. I, for one, wouldn't take the risk of employing a British tradesman in Spain again.

It Was the Binoculars That Did It

Not only had we been foolish with initially choosing Tony as our builder in El Nacarino, we also eventually discovered we'd fallen foul of an expat keyholder.

Before we got rid of Tony, we had a message from him while we were in England to say he'd left our key with Sandra, a lady in the next village. The intention was to collect the key on our next trip over but by then she'd phoned me, told me she'd been in and had a tidy round, and that she ran a key-holding service, looking after several houses in the area. We met eventually; I liked Sandra — a lot — so we decided to leave the key with her. Her husband, Jimmy, was a handyman and could do odd jobs for us when needed so it seemed an ideal situation.

Over the next couple of years, we became firm friends. Sandra was good to us and the house was superbly maintained. But then the big bills started to come in. We began to get outrageous electricity bills for times when we weren't there and unexpected maintenance bills. These were always explained away as them testing the heating for when we were next over, a problem that needed fixing, a job that

Jimmy had to do, or that Jimmy had to paint something and it took her seven hours to clean after him. Always a ready and plausible answer. Every time I looked at Jimmy, he had his hand out for €200. Then Sandra started to phone me to say someone had been in the house and she asked who else had keys.

'I think Sandra's throwing up a smoke screen,' Adrian said after yet another large bill arrived.

'What d'you mean?'

'I reckon she's renting the house out while we're not there.'

'D'you really think she'd do that?' I asked. 'I know you've suspected it for a while but... Would Sandra really do that to us?'

'We can't possibly be incurring the expenses we're being asked to pay for, is all I know.' He looked at me, knowing I'd have to agree despite my reluctance to accept that someone I liked would treat us like this.

Sandra and Jimmy ran a B&B in the next village and Sandra had, on occasion, asked me if I wanted to earn extra money by renting out a room as they'd overbooked and were looking for somewhere to put people. We always refused. It was never our intent to make money on the house so the answer was always the same. This was our home and it wasn't available for rent; it was our personal space and Sandra was very aware we didn't want to go down the rental route. Each time she responded with, 'OK, I'll pop them into Jonno's,' or, 'I'll pop them into Andrea's.' Rather than turning down the booking, she would always find somewhere to accommodate her paying guests.

'Whatever Sandra says when we turn down her rental suggestions,' Adrian added, 'I'm convinced she's renting our house regardless and pocketing the money.'

It was to turn out that he was right.

One day I was in the corner shop and Carmen, our neighbour, told us people were staying in the house when we weren't there. We didn't know many people in Spain at that time and those that we did, Carmen also knew. She was adamant it wasn't any of them. It was people she didn't recognise.

'No, not your friends. I have not seen these people before.'

'Are you sure?' I still hoped Adrian was wrong in his assumption.

'Absolutely. Several times.'

Our estate agent told us Jimmy had approached him to ask if he had viewings over a particular weekend as they had people staying there. He was suspicious but hadn't passed on his concerns because Jimmy had told him he'd cleared it with me first.

On one occasion we arrived late, went to bed, and the bedclothes stank. Under where I was sleeping was a massive sweat stain that soaked through to the mattress cover. Our bed had been slept in and the dirty sheets left on the bed. I questioned Sandra and she looked genuinely puzzled.

'I don't know, Jean. Do you think that other couple, your friends, have used a key and not told you?'

Whatever happened, she had an answer. Food left in cupboards was because Jimmy had noticed we hadn't got something so put it in. 'That will be five euros, please.' It just went on and on but she was my friend, a good friend. She just wouldn't be ripping me off, would she?

What hurt the most when the sudden bolt of realisation hit me was this betrayal. She was my friend and I was sharing with her the odd things that were happening, unexplained things, irrational things, (nobody, but nobody, breaks in to leave a pint of milk), and she was feigning innocence and surprise, and pretending to know nothing. In my already fragile mental state, I thought I was losing my mind and she let me believe I was imagining things. How cruel can you get?

Over time as things started to disappear, I seriously began to question my mental functioning. I didn't question that my friend would do this to me. Why would I? I trusted her and was confiding in her. Adrian was suspicious of her and I defended her. Did I imagine the binoculars were missing, for example? Did we ever really bring them over? I was doubting myself all the time, sure I'd made a mistake and that missing things would eventually turn up. Lightbulbs went missing from my dresser and turned up in bedside lamps in a room we didn't use; the washing machine, always set at 700 revs because of vibration, was turned up to 1000 revs and was soaking wet inside. Because we were only occasional visitors, to prevent mould I always dried it completely and left the door ajar. I knew I hadn't left it wet.

Even then I was willing to think Sandra might have just 'popped something in' while she was there. Despite the obvious, I still wasn't prepared to believe my friend would lie to me and take such advantage of me.

We met for tapas with Jimmy and Sandra one day and I mentioned the missing binoculars. The look that went between them said everything. The light finally came on and my heart sank. They knew exactly where the binoculars had gone. In fact they knew everything and they'd been caught out. The self-delusion came crashing in on me. What a fool I'd been. I felt humiliated, hurt, and unbelievably stupid.

Adrian had been right. They *were* thieving bastards.

Living la Vida Loca

Life in Spain was different in unexpected ways. Obviously there was sunshine and the language was different but there were many other differences, some subtle and some not so. A traffic jam in El Nacarino usually meant a herd of goats was up ahead, blocking the way for cars and pedestrians. Everything stopped for goats. Seeing the herd coming, weaving its way in and out of, and clambering over, everything in its way was a sight I would never tire of. It filled me with absolute delight every time.

Spain even smelt different. In El Nacarino it would sometimes be the cinnamon smell of the *mantecados* biscuits (which are a little like shortbread in texture) hanging heavily in the air or the olives, with their freshly mown grass bouquet. At other times the wonderful aroma of food wafted from the neighbours' houses, sometimes smelling so mouth-wateringly good that we were tempted to invite ourselves to lunch. Sometimes the air in that hillside town was so clear and clean and sweet that it purged the soul of any ill.

The pace of life in El Nacarino was different too. People

went to work, raised families, cooked, cleaned, and went about their business the same as everyone else but, although the noise levels made it seem frenetic, life took on a slower, more relaxed tempo. Everything happened, and nothing happened. Neighbours called out to each other; the knife sharpener came around on his bike calling out his trade; a van toured the streets selling goods out of the back and ringing a large, hand-held bell and yet, somehow, despite the noise, it was peaceful. Even Adrian had started to enjoy his visits.

The Spanish sunshine brings with it a different existence, a life that's lived outdoors. The Spanish people are, in general, more outgoing and gregarious by nature and any event is an excuse for a party. It's Wednesday — let's get together for some food, drink, and music! Only the Spanish could turn a traffic jam into a *fiesta*, a party. Anything and everything are an excuse for fun. Some weeks are just *fiesta* and siesta, stopping only to sleep for a while before starting the party up again with incredible and sustained amounts of energy.

There are saints' days, name days, saints' weeks, Holy Week, village holidays, and every one of them is party time; tradition and folklore that are still so strong and respected. This respect for culture beats strong in every Spanish heart. During these carnivals the streets are full of people; garages and houses open up and become bars stuffed to the seams with people eating, drinking, and having fun; streets are decorated and life takes on a happier, larger dimension. The whole town is involved. One of the most charming and heart-warming sights is seeing the beautiful women in full flamenco dress.

It's not unusual to be passed in the street by men dressed as angels, or fairies, or floor mops. It took some getting used to until I realised there was a party going on in some other part of town and these guys were on their way to join the procession. On one occasion Bill, one of our El Nacarino friends, had a friend over for the unicycling convention. As we got into our car, he suddenly appeared on his cycle and rode in front of us as we drove out of town. He was a huge, bearded guy and the dichotomy of him on a shocking pink unicycle as he rode sedately in front of us was hugely funny.

There had been a carnival going on in the next street to us since Friday, making parking and sleep very difficult. There was a fairground, sideshows, and a proliferation of bars opening up in garages and basements with parties going on until the early hours. On the Sunday morning, Adrian and I were taking the opportunity of a lull in the activity and enjoying a nice, peaceful, relaxed morning when I heard music starting up again — loud, rhythmic, processionary type music, and this time very close by. I rushed out onto the balcony to see a lot of people milling around at the end of the street. This was unusual in our part of El Nacarino. Apart from the chatter of neighbours and the drone of the occasional dratted moped that Spanish youth are so fond of, nothing much happened in our neighbourhood. I hurried outside for a closer look, just in time to see our first ever procession, *La Octava de los Remedios*, Our Lady of the Remedies.

Our area of El Nacarino was known as *los Remedios* and this particular virgin was ours or, rather, we were hers and, thus, very special to the locality. She appeared, in splendiferous form, on her platform carrying a small child. We watched the virgin and child carried along Calle San Fernando, past the end of Royale and down into the narrowest of alleys then down the steep hill into Calle Lucio to start her procession through the town, the music from the municipal band, *Los Amigos de Música del Nacarino*, delightfully out of tune but playing with real dedication and vigour, escorting her on the journey. Hundreds of Nacariños thronged around her, completely and tightly filling the narrow streets.

The excitement of the procession was intense; people were buzzing. Small boys dressed as altar servers with their red cassocks and white lacy surplices swung fragrant incense in silver thuribles, purifying and sanctifying, taking the prayers of the faithful up to heaven. Older boys in white cassocks belted with gold cord carried tall, silver crosses while girls, from tiny babies to older women, wore flamenco dresses, their raven hair adorned with flowers. The population of El Nacarino were there in their very best clothes, their beloved and revered virgin on the shoulders of 70 strong men.

The virgin and child were wearing gold robes, heavily encrusted with jewels and embroidery. The float was a work of art. Spectacular and also gold, adorned with flowers, carvings, and angels to see the virgin and child safely on their way, it weighed over 2,000 kilos. The bearers walked close together in each other's footsteps, carrying the virgin and child around the town, walking to the beat of the music and stopping every few yards to put the float gently on the ground and rest for a while.

Carmen, one of our neighbours, came up beside me, slipped her arm around me and hugged me, kissing me on top of my head, pleased to see me taking part. A few minutes later, she took my hand and gently led me inside the church. Despite it being attached to the house, I'd never been inside. It was breathtaking! I gasped at the gold-lined walls, so incredibly ornate; at the simple, but beautiful, altar, the statues, and the icons. I've been inside churches in England but I've never seen anything like this. This tiny church, so unimposing from the outside, was a treasure trove; the only other colours were the enamel stations of the cross and the wooden pews; everything else, everywhere, was dazzling, shiny, eye-spiking gold.

We were fond of our little church, despite never previously going inside. It was a nice landmark, joining two streets, attached to the first house in each one. When the bells rang, there was a whoosh through the house as they swung backwards and forwards. We called it the Mickey and Minnie Church as the bells had decorative tops that looked like huge Mickey Mouse ears and were comical swinging side by side. We could never have imagined the treasure hiding within.

We joined the procession and followed it for a while, the street rammed with people, more standing on decorated and draped balconies, some throwing rose petals onto the virgin as she passed. After about an hour, we reached the end of the street just a few hundred yards from where we started. Instead of going into the church, the procession turned into the road at the side of it and started the parade through the town. By now we'd seen enough and decided to return home.

It was evening by the time Adrian and I decided to venture out again, this time to get some food. As we reached the end of Calle Solares, the procession was still in full swing and the virgin was coming back towards us on the other side of the church, having completed her tour around the town. We stopped and, as we watched the procession come to an end, the road closed behind us in readiness for the fireworks that were about to come. We'd seen marks chalked into the road earlier but, as the traffic continued as normal, we thought no more of them. Huge cakes of multi-shot fireworks interspersed with rockets and fountains now appeared and were placed on the chalk marks. The virgin reached the door of the church and was turned around to face the fireworks to watch the display.

Rockets shot high above us and exploded in vibrant,

cascading colours into the night sky. Golden fountains sprang from the pavement and the barrages and cakes whizzed and banged and shot stars and chrysanthemums up into the air. It was exciting, exhilarating, and spectacular. Adrian leant towards me and said, 'I think you should move.'

Because El Nacarino is built into the side of a hill, every street was higher or lower than the next. At the end of Solares were steps down to the next street. I was sitting on the wall at the top of the steps to watch the display. A look over my shoulder showed me I was about to become part of the entertainment and not just an onlooker. The rails around the steps I was leaning on were covered with Catherine wheels and rockets.

I moved!

There were no barriers, no warning signs, and dozens of people crowding around. When the fireworks went off, people oohed and aaahed in close sizzling distance of them, completely unfazed by any danger. As the smoke cleared in the narrow street, we could see people leaning over their balconies watching the fireworks, right on top of where these explosives had been ignited.

Suddenly a crackle came from behind us as another display began. This was the finale in the unguarded doorway of the church. Silver and gold fountains rained down on the blessed virgin and child to see them into the church. Then, as the fireworks ended and the sparkles faded, she was turned and, in the smoke remaining, disappeared through the door of the church.

It had been magnificent, extravagant, brilliant, dangerous; the wonderful display vividly demonstrating how alive and happy El Nacarino was that night, the perilous fire hazard and risk of serious burns overlooked and inconsequential, safety precautions non-existent, the road only being closed to prevent cars spoiling the display.

A week later we were driving along and looked open-mouthed at a dumper truck coming towards us. In the bucket were five children. Health and safety in Spain? You're joking, right?

El Nacarino

El Nacarino is a beautiful little town which we loved but the house there was only ever going to be a stepping stone towards getting what we eventually wanted. The lack of outside space, just the tiniest patio surrounded by walls, was always going to be a problem. It was lovely to sit there in the cool of the morning for breakfast but there was nowhere to put a lounger and relax in the sun.

This was defeating one of the principal reasons for having a house in Spain. It was restrictive and we sweltered through the hot summer on days when we should have been outside. A day in the sun meant a trip to the local pool or a drive to the lakes. Most of the houses around were the same. The Spanish, not being sunseekers like the rest of northern Europe, stayed indoors during the heat of the day and would bring chairs out into the street in the evening. That is their social time. In every Spanish town, people spill out into the streets and live life outside. In El Nacarino the pavements weren't designed for pedestrians, some being less than twelve inches wide, so the chairs were in the road. This made it difficult for cars in the narrow streets but the residents didn't seem to mind. Nobody moved and no cars slowed down.

The narrow streets weren't designed for cars but are jam-packed with both cars and pedestrians, especially in the lower part of town. Apart from siesta time, which is sacrosanct, the town is constantly on the move and always changing. In our time in El Nacarino, we watched the restoration of monuments, the development of the factories, and the building of new houses. Unfortunately, many of these houses were begun just as the property market in Spain crashed and they remain half finished. One house, which promised to be stunning, has been left as a shell. The outside brick frame is there but there are no walls, no staircases, just daylight. Bizarrely, the swimming pool is complete and filled and ready for use. There are streetlights, the roads are laid, and there are other structures around that have been started and left. It's a sad part of town. A ghost town on the edge of a thriving community.

The thing about Spain is there is no volume control. Without doubt Spain has to be one of the noisiest countries on the planet. The Spanish nature is to be gregarious, outgoing, sociable. Loud. TVs blare out of houses at maximum volume; dogs bark; cars rev; silencers are taken out of mopeds. If the neighbour at number four is chatting to the neighbour at number thirty, neither move from their respective doorsteps; they just shout up the street to each other. When we first arrived in Spain, we thought someone was arguing outside the house. It was two women discussing lunch. Food, along with fun and flamenco, is taken seriously in Spain. One of the three Fs that are very important to a balanced life.

El Nacarino is one of the white towns of Andalusia and built on a hill, the Cerro San Pedro. The higher you get in the town, the less busy it is and the more beautiful with winding, cobbled streets, whitewashed houses, cherished monuments, churches. Parts of the town are breathtaking — if you have any breath left to take after scaling those steep streets, that is. Many's the time I was left gasping, heart thumping, muscles bursting, but feeling full of wonder when I reached the top of the town. The effort was always worth it. We had eight years in El Nacarino and, every time we went out for a walk, we found something new.

Noisy, bustling, dusty, I loved it!

At the top of the hill is the Santa Lucia convent and the Balcón de Andalucía, the balcony of Andalusia. On one side there is a quarry. A huge scar in the landscape but, perhaps surprisingly, not unpleasant to look at. On the other, from the Balcón, you can see forever. And forever is beautiful, looking out over El Nacarino, stretching out over the Sevillian plains, dotted with pretty whitewashed villages, and on a clear day, into Córdoba, Malaga, and the Sierra de Granada. After the climb we would get our breath back, only to lose it again at the sight of the stunning vista in front of us. Yes, El Nacarino is beautiful.

It tumbles down the Cerro San Pedro like a beanbag spilling its contents. There's a fluidity to it which spreads in all directions downwards from the convent and the Santa Teresa church. It isn't difficult to find on a map. If you draw lines to criss-cross Andalusia, right at the centre, where the lines meet, you would find El Nacarino. The heart of Andalusia. This heart beats with a strong pulse.

The town is still affluent, vibrant, colourful. Despite the current economic climate, El Nacarino prospers and the unemployment rate is very low. The major industries are *mantecados, polvorones*, and olive oil. Factories produce the *mantecados*, a type of very soft shortbread that's made using pig fat (*manteca*), but much of the industry is home-based. The majority of these biscuits are sold for Christmas and, on the run-up to Christmas, the smell of cinnamon and spices permeates the town with a wonderful sweetness. To me, they're an acquired taste, somewhat akin to sickly sweet sawdust with overtones of pig, and they smell a lot better than they taste, but the Spanish love them and El Nacarino is one of the Andalusian towns famous for them.

Mantecados and *polvorones* are similar. One is a cake, the other is shortbread but, to me, they both taste about the same. *Polvorone* comes from the Spanish word for dust, *polvo*, and these biscuits are meant to crumble to dust. To stop them crumbling, it's customary to squish them into a firmer piece before putting them into the mouth. It doesn't make them more palatable but it does prevent a lot of mess!

Surrounding El Nacarino are olive trees as far as the eye can see. They smell a little like freshly cut grass and their delicate scent hangs in the air. From early October until February, there's an almost constant procession of tractors and trucks along the Avenida, El Nacarino's main road, into the co-operative for pressing.

El Nacarino produces some of the finest olive oil in Spain, rated one of the world's best oils of 2016. The different times for harvesting the olives depend on whether they're for eating or for oil. The green ones are the first to be picked; the black ones, the last. When they're turning purple, just before they fully ripen, is when they're at their richest in oil. Olives are big business and, at picking time, no matter what else people are doing, everyone downs tools and goes to help. No part of the olive is wasted. At the mill the liquid is separated from the solids and the solids then go on to form animal feed or pellets for burners. Everything gets used.

El Nacarino is a very ancient town with a very disturbing history. It was founded by the Carthaginians who were in Spain from 575 BC to 206 BC when the Romans defeated them. There was a lot of toing and froing between different conquerors and then, during the Punic Wars with Rome, El Nacarino took the side of the Carthaginians. When the victorious Romans finally invaded the town in 208BC, they found the inhabitants had burned their possessions and committed suicide rather than live under Roman rule. The Romans repopulated the town, renamed it, and lived there for 400 years until they were ejected by the Visigoths, who then ruled there until overrun by the Moorish armies in the eighth century. From then it changed hands several times as various armies attempted to take control of this important outpost until, finally, it was taken by King Ferdinand III in 1241. From that time onwards, the town has thrived.

Each era has left its mark. Standing atop the hill, alongside the convent and church, are the restored remains of the pre-Roman castle which had been renovated by the Moors. The ancient town wall surrounds the area. Down in the town are the mansions of the Dukes of Arcos and beautifully maintained 15th-century churches. Historic sites are well preserved. You could justifiably put a canopy over El Nacarino and make one of the biggest museums in the world.

We had the most amazing neighbours in El Nacarino and their friendship was appreciated more than they could ever have known. Many was the time, in the early days while the renovations were taking place, that I would go over to Spain on my own. As soon as I arrived, the neighbours would come to see me; offers of help were always there and their kindness knew no bounds. Rosa from next door would come to chat; Marta's door, opposite, was always open; Carmen, who worked in the corner shop, would phone for her daughter to help me with my clumsy Spanish; and Concha, darling Concha, whom I lost my heart to, reminded me so much of my beloved grandmother whom I loved and have missed all of my adult life. She filled a space that had been empty for so long. I may have been on my own but I was never alone.

As was customary in the town, we kept the front door open during the day. This allowed the flow of air through the house and easy access for neighbours and friends to call in. It wasn't unusual, while the renovations were taking place, for casual passersby to stop, look in, and even occasionally step inside, to point out the work that had been done and the changes made. If we were sitting on a sofa they would say, '*Hola,*' and carry on looking, animatedly chatting, pointing, and sometimes passing encouraging comments. The Spanish are curious by nature and these Nacariños were enchantingly uninhibited in satisfying their curiosity.

Thank you, El Nacarino. You gave me so much and a big piece of my heart will always remain with you.

A Different World

One of the things I've struggled to come to terms with since buying property in Spain is the difference in how the Spanish use time. Take siesta, for example. English shops have long since stopped closing for lunch. However, in Spain, nearly everything — shops, offices, factories — closes at two and doesn't open again until five. Banks don't open again in the afternoon at all.

Any business needs to be transacted in the morning and, given how the Spanish love to turn everything into a social occasion, it means getting up early. Long queues form as last night's TV gets discussed, uncle's hernia is chewed over, the cousin's wedding is dissected. Everyone knows everyone and these conversations are lengthy and involved. Then, just as you think it's over and you can move up a place, something else is remembered and it starts all over again. Grocery shopping is a little easier as the trend these days is for the big supermarkets to stay open all day but, if you don't have one of those nearby, you're scuppered until five when siesta time is over.

Another thing is meal times. When we first arrived, we

wandered down to the restaurant nearby at seven and found
it shut. At the time this was the only restaurant we knew of
in El Nacarino so, disappointed and hungry, we turned around
and wandered back up the hill, through the town, looking for
somewhere else to eat. There was nowhere. By the time we
got back home, it was almost eight and, not having eaten
since breakfast, we were ravenous. The fridge didn't hold
anything tempting so we got in the car and went out to find
somewhere. As we drove past the restaurant again, there was
a glimmer of light from deep within. The bar, at least, was
open. We went in.

'Are you open?'

'*Sí.*' Yes.

'Ah, good. Can we eat here?'

'*Sí, claro.*' Of course.

'May we order?'

'*No.*'

They laid a table for us and directed us to the bar where
we ordered drinks; beer for Adrian, white wine for me. On an
empty stomach, this could be a mistake. At nine a skinny,
turbaned woman sailed past us into the kitchen and the lights
went on. This was promising.

A waiter led us to our table and another round of drinks
appeared. By 9:30 p.m., and slightly squiffy, we were able to
order. We were still the only people in the restaurant, the
only other patron having left his barstool some time
previously. By ten, people started to drift in and I
remembered we'd come by car. I never, but never, drink and
drive. I don't take a sip of alcohol if I'm about to get behind a
steering wheel. I don't even reach for the keys but this time
I'd forgotten. Two glasses of wine on an empty stomach
wasn't a good thing. The realisation and shock sobered my
thoughts quickly and we considered the options. One, I could
drink myself sober (kidding!) Two, we could stay until I was

safe to drive and, three, we could walk home. We went for option two.

The restaurant started to fill up and, by eleven, it was standing room only. They were setting up extra tables in any odd corners they could find. Children were running around and the noise was escalating to jack-hammer level. All the time the television was blaring away in the background, no one taking a blind bit of notice. Barcelona were playing someone or other. Who knew who? Who cared? It just added to the noise and atmosphere.

At midnight people were still coming in; grannies, mums bumping prams down the entrance steps, children (who should be in school the next morning) and toddlers running riot.

With typical English reserve, we were starting to feel guilty at hogging a table for so long so, at one o'clock and feeling safe to drive, we got up to leave. No one had pressured us; there were no awkward stares but it just felt wrong to take up such much-needed space. As we left, a family of eight slipped around our tiny table. The night was still young.

We reflected that, back in Essex, by now an impatient waiter would be trying to rush us out, someone would be whipping a Hoover around our feet, the table would have been cleared away (whether everyone had finished eating or not) and someone would have been standing by the door, anxious to lock up as soon as we'd been hurried outside.

Yes, Spain is different.

'If you need anything for the children, come and see me. You need milk? I have milk.'

We'd arrived late and the journey from Seville airport had been a difficult one. This was the first time we'd flown into

Seville and I'd got lost, ending up in the centre of the city with its one-way streets and myriad of blind alleys. It had been almost five hours since we'd got off the plane. My daughter Suzanne and grandchildren Findley and Eva were all tired. It was nearly ten o'clock and my neighbours, as was customary, were all sitting out in the street. Marta was concerned for the children.

'Knock on my door if you need anything,' she insisted.

The Spanish love of children is legendary. In any family they take first place. They are doted on, adored, revered, pampered, and spoiled, and they grow into very nice, confident adults because of it. It matters not whether it's the child of the family or a stranger; every child is awarded the same treatment. When Eva was a baby, a walk into town would take forever as passersby ooohed and aaahed into the pram. Complete strangers would cross the road to pat and fuss the baby. Other young mums with prams would be called over to compare notes.

Children in Spain grow up secure in the knowledge that they're an accepted, integral, and important part of the family and community. If we were out in the street with the grandchildren, grannies with grandchildren would pop out of houses to allow us to coo in mutual appreciation of the various beloved offspring. There were times when the street resembled a crèche. The only risk to our children in El Nacarino was they might have disappeared into a neighbouring doorway and been loved to death.

On one occasion we heard raucous laughter from outside and went to investigate. There, on our balcony, was Findley, stark naked, performing a dance routine to a very appreciative audience.

Christian, my daughter Chrystal's son, is the oldest grandchild and it was safe to allow him out on his own when he was still young. The babies were the biggest pull so

Christian, at ten, didn't have quite the same draw. He would go to the corner shop opposite for bread and come back with handfuls of sweets.

'Why did you buy those, Christian?'

'I didn't. My friend gave them to me.'

His friend was Carmen, the shop manager.

Going anywhere in a hurry was a non-starter. If we needed to go somewhere quickly, we would look up and down the street, wait until it was empty, and make a dash for the car. I wouldn't have had my warm-hearted, generous-natured neighbours any other way.

What surprised us was the obsession Spanish housewives have for cleaning. There are some pretty dilapidated properties in the towns and on our search for a house we'd been into some fully furnished dustbins and some greasy hovels but, while there are plenty of these around, they're the exception rather than the rule. Part of Adrian's resistance to Spain came from the fact he'd never been there before without getting some serious tummy upsets. Often it seemed as if his tummy started to gurgle as he was walking down the aircraft steps. We'd had some pretty grim times. Many years previously, in Menorca, the food poisoning was so bad there was a risk he wouldn't be allowed to fly home. He was, understandably, somewhat hesitant about visiting and it took him a while to get on board with my dream of a life in the sun. On his first visit to El Nacarino, his suitcase was so full of Diocalm that I debated whether it was worth buying shares.

Inland, the hygiene standards were so different from the coastal areas. We eat in restaurants and bars and there has never been a problem. If a place doesn't look up to scratch, we give it a miss but, to be honest, these places are few and far between. It's amazing the difference a few thousand tourists can make to your well-being. In most Spanish towns, the streets are clean. Junk mail doesn't come through the post but is hand delivered, sometimes put in letterboxes, sometimes tucked under knockers, and sometimes just shoved through cracks in doors or the bars over the windows. This inevitably leads to reams of it blowing its way through the streets. On leaflet day in El Nacarino, the roads are a mess. The following day it's all gone. The leaflet fairy cleans it all away and the women are straight out with their mops and buckets, washing down the pavements. Window bars are dusted, doors are wiped, brass is polished, and life carries on. Spick and span again.

Adrian's fond memory of El Nacarino is the smell of disinfectant.

The KKK?

As I walked past a photographer's shop near the town hall in El Nacarino one day, I was horrified to see a photo of the Ku Klux Klan in the window and, beside it, a model of a Klansman — pointy hat, head to toe in white, with a cross on his chest. It was so unexpected and shocking that it took my breath away. I wanted to walk on by and not look but the photo and revolting statue had my attention. I stood, transfixed, for a moment wide-eyed and slack-jawed in horror.

Soon afterwards, I visited La Rambla, a small town about an hour's drive from El Nacarino. A sleepy little town, quite unimposing, and not very pretty as Spanish towns go, it's famous for its pottery and was a favourite trip for me and my daughter Chrystal. There are row upon row of shops selling ceramics of all sorts, from religious icons to the avant-garde. Pots of all shapes and sizes are stacked outside in colourful heaps and there's a constant supply of new ceramics fed in by the factories that make up the main industry of the area.

On a visit to buy some hand-painted plates, we were drawn into a shop by the heady scent of incense. Inside there was an instant sense of calm, the shop filled with the comforting, sweet-smelling aroma of churches. Separate from the vibrant display of plates and dishes, among statues of the Madonna, wooden crosses, and religious ornaments, were rows of KKK; whole armies of them, in different colours, lined up in regiments and looking so out of place in this holy area.

'What are these?' I asked the man behind the counter.

'*Señora*, they are *Nazarenos*. Very special,' he said as he took one, lit an incense tablet, and popped it inside.

Then it dawned. These were not Klan; they were incense burners and had a strong religious significance. This shop, with its peaceful and kind ambience, was selling not Klansmen but *Nazarenos*, models of Penitents atoning for the death of Christ.

Here endeth the first lesson: Do not jump to conclusions. Things are not always what they seem.

During Holy Week there are processions every day, each one of them different. The procession of the Penitents is one of the more spectacular and, possibly, the most spine-chilling. The Penitents are completely covered, with long robes, capirotes (tall pointy hats), and a white cowl with eyeholes covering their faces. The robes and capirotes give them anonymity as they walk in formation through the streets, the intention being that only God knows who they are, protecting the identity of the sinners. The standard colour for robes is white although different brotherhoods will frequently use different colours, each having a special meaning. It is, without doubt, an awesomely beautiful sight and intensely emotional; the devotion and passion of those watching and taking part are incredible.

My first sight of the Penitents as they came out of the church is difficult to describe, such were the emotions it stirred in me. As the doors opened, the Penitents stood there silent and majestic, beautiful and yet, at the same time, sinister. Hooded and haunting, they completely took my breath away. It was an awesome mixture of shock, amazement at the beauty, anger, reverent emotion, and a strange feeling of shame.

They stood there immobile, quieting the crowd outside to a respectful murmur. Onlookers prayed, heads bowed. Some crossed themselves; some looked straight ahead, spellbound; some just talked quietly to their neighbour. And then a slow drum beat escorted them out of the church.

After the first few Penitents, a huge cross was carried with a life-size effigy of Christ. The music that accompanied it was mournful, almost funereal. I suppose, in a way, that's exactly what it was. With the crucifix and Christ being carried at the front, it's the devoted, dignified, and respectful funeral that He was denied in life.

The procession around the town took several hours and carried on until the early hours of the morning, the pious in their heavy robes and capirotes. Many of them were barefoot and wore shackles as they walked in silence, carrying candles or crosses. At night time the candles were lit, giving the procession an even more haunting and sinister look.

The capirote is a mark of humility and points skywards so the penance reaches closer to heaven. It's a powerful image and there were times during this procession that I felt the emotions overwhelming. I was born Methodist, married a Catholic, and took the girls to church when they were young but, if I'm honest, religion hasn't played too big a part in my life so I was surprised at this cascade of feelings, some of it joy and some of it intense revulsion.

Even knowing this was a demonstration of deep devotion, I was uncomfortable with it and still found it disconcerting when, in the evening, a whole horde of Penitents, all in white, came plodding determinedly, silently, and doggedly towards me. Despite its beauty, it was also sinister and the burning candles made me shudder. En masse I found the Penitents frightening and menacing. It was so sad that this homage that was paid with such piety, seen through the wrong eyes, just brought a feeling of terror.

Yet it was an awe-inspiring sight and I wanted to appreciate it; I really did. It was beautiful and it was frightening; it provoked deep-seated emotions and humility; it was glorious and it was repulsive and it left me very confused.

In the back of my mind were some awful images that robbed the day of any benign and holy influences. I remembered seeing television reports of white-robed supremacists burning crosses and carrying out vile and murderous acts in America. I shuddered at that as a child. It still makes me shudder today. Without doubt the Klan have ruined something beautiful. Centuries of tradition have been sullied. The anti-Catholic KKK have stolen the robes and capirotes of a peaceful and contrite offering and made it represent something evil. Maybe they believe it gives legitimacy to their brand of malevolence. It doesn't. All it does is gives them anonymity while they carry out cowardly acts. I can't erase those images from my mind. I can't unsee what I've seen and where I saw it first. I saw it before I saw the marvel and devotion of these Penitents.

The image of burning crosses and evil doers in the deep south is too firmly imprinted in my mind and, at this present time, the Klan, frighteningly, appear to be making a resurgence in some places.

With my blood running cold, I'm afraid the Penitents' procession is never going to be top of my must-see list.

Perhaps not at night anyway.

Selling Up

Adrian had never been entirely happy in El Nacarino and didn't want to spend any length of time there. The longest visit he made was two weeks and that was only because he'd broken his ribs and needed looking after. If I was going to get him out to Spain more often, it was clear the house in El Nacarino was going to be time-limited. It had always been the original plan to move on to something that suited us better so the decision was taken to put the house on the market. John and Shirley had long since lost interest in the property and I'd bought out Shirley's share so the house was completely ours. They were much happier by the coast close to her sister where the beer was apparently better. Adrian was happy to go off-roading without John and we were both relieved not to have anyone else to consider in our use of the house.

Altogether the renovations had taken over two years but we'd completely renewed the house. We were very proud of how smart and pretty it was. It was light, airy, and very comfortable. In any other market, I don't believe we would have had any trouble selling it. However, by the time it was ready to sell, the property bubble had burst and the house was to remain on the market for another five years.

Estate agents in Spain at the time were, by and large, a pretty shifty lot and there appeared to be few controls over their shoddy behaviour and absolutely *no* controls over the amount of commission they charged. It ranged from a standard set commission to any number they could pluck out of the air at the time. The only consistent number was zero; they tagged lots of them onto the number they first thought of.

We had visits from the spivs, the wide boys, and the condescending idiots who looked down their noses at what we had to offer. One over-the-hill, overly made-up, mini-skirted dolly bird waltzed into the house smoking a cigarette and proceeded to clack her stilettos around the place while wafting trails of stale smoke behind her before using photos from another agent's site and banging a whopping €32,000 commission on top of the asking price. We never heard from her again and she never did show anyone round. Unsurprisingly, when the property market crashed, she was one of the first to go out of business. Another agent listed our house but never visited; instead he asked me to send photos which he then used on his own site to advertise El Nacarino as a place of interest to visit.

During the time the house was on the market, there was a lot of interest but no offers. We had genuine house hunters and we had day-trippers, people who had nothing better to do on a weekend than to come and nose around someone else's house. We stressed to everyone that there was only a minute patio but still they came and complained there was no outside space. One lady even arrived with two dogs, one of them a Great Dane. We listened to all of the feedback and tried to change wherever possible to meet the need.

We were amazed people couldn't look past what was in

front of them and envision their furniture in the house. One refusal was because we didn't have any wardrobes. We weren't selling the furniture but, OK, it was flagged as an issue so we bought some. Someone else didn't like a shower curtain so we took it out and installed glass sliding doors. One by one, as issues arose, we ticked them off. The one we couldn't overcome easily was the lack of outside space and the fact the bathroom was downstairs. We didn't want to spend any more money but there was nothing for it; we would have to bite the bullet and have a roof terrace added.

Having had major problems with the previous English builder, we employed Paco who had unbotched the previous English cowboy's handiwork. We told him what we wanted and he applied for licences, planning permission, and had an architect draw up the plans. He told us when he would start, when he would finish, and gave us a written estimate in advance of how much it would all cost. All of which he kept to, presenting us at the end with a superb new roof, terrace, upstairs bathroom, and a very stylish spiral staircase.

Paco was a small, neat, courteous man with a twinkle in his eye. Sometimes he would arrive with his daughter, sometimes with his wife, and sometimes with his mistress. At other times there would be any combination of the three, Paco always being the constant. No one seemed at all concerned by the girlfriend's presence, least of all Señora Paco. I have no idea if this is common practice in Spain but it didn't seem anything out of the ordinary in this family. It took some getting used to but we reasoned that, if the family weren't bothered, then we shouldn't be either.

We liked Paco. It was hard not to. He was hardworking, honest, and trustworthy, and always very proper despite his unusual domestic arrangement. He was friendly, if a little sombre, but that twinkle gave the impression there was always something a little mischievous bubbling away below the surface.

Along with Paco came Austin, a larger-than-life character, big in stature and personality, with a laugh that could be heard in the next village. Jovial and kind-hearted, nothing was too much trouble. Austin is an Englishman, permanently resident in Spain and, for a very minimal fee, he project-managed the building work. He arranged storage of our furniture while the roof was off, ensured the correct payments were made at the right time, and kept us informed of progress. This was extremely useful when the building inspector was trying to overturn the already approved architect's plans.

Plan? What plan? This was Spain and official plans meant nothing and nothing was straightforward. The alterations may have been architect designed, the plans may have been approved by the town council and the Provincial Council of Seville, but the building inspector said no and, if the building inspector says no, it's just not going to happen.

'You are not allowed a bedroom on the roof; the treads on the spiral staircase are too wide; move that wall eighteen inches this way, no, back that way a foot, no, forward a foot.'

I lost count of the times Paco re-built the back wall until the final time he was told to move it again. This time he nodded and did nothing. The next time the inspector came, it was approved. We were so grateful Austin and Paco had that headache and not us.

When we decided to add the roof terrace, we also decided to take the house off the market. The new bathroom meant an upstairs bedroom was lost but there was an oversized corridor downstairs just off the original bathroom that converted into a single bedroom with en-suite facilities. It was all rather grand.

Austin ran an odds and ends sort of company looking

after expats, project managing, key holding, and dabbling in a bit of real estate here and there. His company was called 'Here to Help' and he meant it. No matter how big or how small the problem, he was always on hand to help and there are a lot of expats in Andalusia who've had their transition to a new life made easier with his assistance. We all need to be needed to some extent and, maybe, that's partly Austin's motivation but his generosity of spirit is his main driving force. He's a good egg.

With the renovations complete and the much-needed outside space available, we were happier to stay in El Nacarino and there was no rush to sell. There were no plans to remarket the house immediately but I left it with Austin not to forget us if he came across anyone interested. Despite the current contentment, we would still be open to offers.

Having a roof terrace opened up new worlds. We would sit up there listening to the sound of goats passing by at the top of the town, their bells tinkling and the sound of their bleating mingling with the bray of a donkey in the distance drifting in on the breeze. Occasionally a horse would clip-clop down the street, its hooves clattering on the metalled road. Somewhere a lone dog barked and the sound of neighbours' chatter drifted up, close but somehow distant. It had the dreamy, nostalgic feel of holidays of days gone by. It felt different. It felt 'abroad'. One evening I looked across and saw my neighbour flamenco dancing on her roof. The sights, sounds, and smells of Spain, the 'real' Spain, were all there in our tiny universe in El Nacarino.

One day Chrystal and I were sitting on the roof and the wonderful smell of someone's lunch drifted up to us, making our mouths water. Salivating at the tantalising aroma, we breathed deeply and could almost taste it. We felt like Bisto kids following our noses. It smelt so delicious that we envied its future recipient; someone was in for a treat. There were no restaurants nearby so we knew it had to be a neighbour who just had to be an excellent cook. The surprise came later when we wandered down to the kitchen and discovered this tempting smell was coming from my oven — chicken in a Knorr cook-in-sauce bag.

At home in the UK, I've often walked behind people in shops and supermarkets, gagging at the wafts of BO and stale cigarettes. One particular day, in the week before we left for Spain, I was trying to get into a well-known frozen food store. I battled my way through a gaggle of smokers hanging around the door outside, through the fug of cigarette smoke, and straight into someone's fart. Sometimes the fragrances don't compare too favourably. Give me El Nacarino any day.

Moving On

In the softening light of the early evening, the setting sun turned the hills above the house golden. Below, the view stretched away over the plains of Seville and, as night fell, lights dotted here and there twinkled in the villages in the distance. Evenings on the roof terrace were a magical time and I never tired of the view in either direction. We would lie back at night and, when we weren't watching the stars, would watch the planes flying in. There was a certain point where their lights would come on and we could see where they were heading. A left turn meant Malaga, straight on for Granada, and higher up in the sky showed they were going to strange and mysterious places further away. Maybe to Africa, maybe beyond.

A balmy evening, a glass of wine, plane spotting. Simple pleasures. One of my most cherished memories is of a magical night my grandson Findley and I lay sharing a lounger until the early hours, watching shooting stars.

A few months later, Austin was working more or less full time for a pukka estate agent and wasted no time in showing people around our house. Within a very short while, we had an offer. It fell through but it was encouraging. At last we had something that people wanted. It was saleable.

One Saturday morning Adrian and I were in the UK, having a lie-in, when the phone rang.

'Jean, I have an offer on your house.' Austin's voice is distinctive and I recognised it immediately. What he was saying, however, was completely alien and unexpected and, in my sleep-befuddled state, it wasn't sinking in.

'What? Sorry, um, yes, sorry.' Bleary-eyed and fighting sleep, I tried to sound intelligent and Austin laughed as he tried to remain professional, clearly aware I wasn't altogether with it but not wanting to let on to his client.

It was the sort of call that wakes you up quickly but I doubt I was making a lot of sense. We managed to agree a price, which included the furniture, and a quick completion date. Was that it? The call was over in a couple of minutes and it seemed we had struck a deal.

'I think we've sold the house!'

The news shocked Adrian awake. It seemed a lot to take in and very difficult to believe. We'd tried for five long years to sell and now, when we weren't trying, it had sold. Austin had worked a miracle.

We'd previously agreed that, if it made a difference to a sale, we would sell the house fully furnished. There were some personal items we wanted to keep and some decorative bits and pieces we particularly liked but we were prepared to walk away and leave everything else behind. In the end that was what clinched it. The buyer was deciding between two houses and ours won the day because we were prepared to include the furniture.

The next few months were a flurry of activity. We needed to pack up whatever personal items we were taking with us as soon as possible, clean the house, and find somewhere else to buy.

We were on the Ryanair website that morning and on a plane to Spain by the end of the week. It was incredible how much stuff we'd accumulated in the eight years we'd been in El Nacarino. There were crateloads of it. Austin arranged for us to store it all in his huge summer room until we needed it again. It took eight trips to move it all, one for each year, the enormous people-carrier we'd hired full to the gunnels each time.

We spent most of March house hunting. Austin took us to see umpteen places, some stunners and some oddities. One house had been broken into and left in an awful mess. A grand piano had been lifted out over a six-foot fence and carried away and the rest of it completely trashed. Another house we went to see we liked enormously. The English lady who owned it was very proud her grandson had once appeared on the *Jeremy Kyle* show, something I might have kept quiet about but she appeared to believe was a valuable selling point. Ultimately the situation with that house was far too complicated and we gave it a miss.

Some of the stories we heard were heartbreaking — properties being sold because of divorce, the loss of a partner, bank foreclosures, and financial hardship. With every house there was a tale to tell, usually one of sorrow. Apart from the house we eventually bought, not a single one we saw had owners moving on to something better. For so many people, the dream had turned sour.

Most of the houses were out in the countryside and all but one had a garden and a swimming pool. A pool was something we'd dreamed of but never imagined that, with our limited budget, we would be able to afford. Eventually it came down to a choice between two houses.

The first wasn't the favourite. The pool area and garden were stunning and there was an orange grove but it was close to the motorway and the traffic was loud. The noise wasn't too intrusive though and we could live with it. The house itself was another matter. 'It had potential', is the best that could be said. It had some nice features but, overall, it was shabby, old-fashioned, and slightly grimy. The dog-chewed furniture, which had seen better days, was included in the price. Bizarrely, frosted glass was in all of the windows. The living room, kitchen, and dining room were all in one; the bathroom was ancient and the master bedroom needed the light on in the middle of the day. It would need a skylight to let in more light. Despite this, with a bit of imagination, it had potential.

The second house, we fell in love with. It was perfect and in immaculate order. It was down a secluded lane with only a few other neighbours. There were two bedrooms in the main house and there were outbuildings with additional accommodation. The huge garden was stuffed with fruit trees, olive trees, colourful flowers, and sweet herbs of rosemary, lavender, and bay. There was a pool, a pergola, a paddock, and lots of seating areas dotted around in secret gardens. It was peaceful and idyllic. This house had been loved and it couldn't be more obvious; it felt happy. It was more than we could have expected in our wildest dreams and, best of all, it could accommodate all of the family together at the same time.

'Come on, while we're on our own, which do you prefer?'

We'd gone to a bar to take a break and mull things over. Austin and Adrian had gone to order coffee and I was alone with Caz, Austin's partner. Woman to woman, 'just between us', conspiratorially — the way women do — Caz wanted me to state the obvious. She already knew where our hearts lay but it had to be said out loud.

'Hand on heart, we both loved the second one,' I told her. 'That's definitely the one we want. The other one's a bit grim and needs a lot of work.'

But then came the bombshell. The house we'd fallen in love with was €60,000 over our budget. We couldn't afford it. There was no way we could put forward what we had to offer; it would be insulting. We'd already sold El Nacarino and we could put some extra towards it but it was nowhere near enough. We'd met the current owners and they were nice people. We couldn't offend them with the paltry sum we had. A cheeky offer is one thing but that was quite a substantial amount and there was no way this would run. It's difficult to describe the mixture of deflation and shock we felt and the disappointment that our expectations and hopes had been built up over something that was quite clearly out of reach.

'Give it a go. Really, it's always worth a try,' Austin insisted.

Adrian and I discussed for a while and discounted that beautiful property completely. Despite the drawbacks of the first house, we would have to settle for second best and make a bid on it. It would take a lot of work and be costly but we could make it presentable. We'd completely reformed the El Nacarino house so we knew what we could do. At the end of March, we would be homeless in Spain and all our goods and chattels were taking up space in Austin's house. A lot of space that, come the summer, he would need.

We put in an offer on the first house, a low offer we thought reasonable, considering the amount of work that was needed. They told us to poke off!

Austin, in the meantime, had been busy, talking with the owners of both houses and wheeler-dealering negotiations. Eventually he phoned to say the bid we'd made was a non-starter but, if we could raise another €2,000, we could have the house we wanted. To say wheeler-dealer isn't intended to do Austin any disservice; there was no dodgy dealing but, with a bit of jiggery-pokery on costs and commissions, he'd managed to negotiate a deal that was acceptable to the vendors. For us, it was an offer that couldn't be refused. It was a buyers' market but we'd underestimated just how much in favour of the buyer the market was balanced. Even so, for a long time afterwards, as much as we couldn't believe our luck, we also felt guilty for almost stealing their house.

That afternoon we set off to sign the contract to buy our new home in Acerico.

A New Home

'No.'

'What do you mean, "no"?'

We'd waited ages to see Francisco, our new solicitor. Sitting comfortably in the soft, squishy leather sofas in his waiting room while we waited to start the process for buying our new house, we'd been lulled into a false sense that it was going to be a good day yet here he was delivering bad news.

'No, you can't buy this house. There is a problem.'

There was no smile, no eye contact, no cheery 'good morning', just the delivery of bad news without any preamble or attempt to soften the blow.

'I told the Richardsons not to buy it. They didn't listen and now I'm telling you not to buy it.'

With sinking hearts we listened as Francisco explained that the ground the house was built on was part of a much larger plot that had been owned by two brothers. They'd built six properties on it but the land was never legally divided. We could buy the house but the gardens were communally owned.

'You will buy the house but you will not own the land. I

told them eight years ago not to buy that house but they didn't listen so I told them they must sort it and they haven't. So I'm telling you not to buy.'

The news was like a hammer blow and left Adrian and I numb. We'd been offered our own little bit of paradise and, now that it was within grasp, it was being snatched away. The beautiful house, the lovely garden, the swimming pool, the serenity of the countryside, all of it slipping beyond reach, the dream shattered.

'There is a solution.' Francisco broke the silence. 'But it's not an easy one. It will take some time and it depends on lots of factors coming into agreement.'

He went on to explain he would write to all the other house owners and, if they agreed to his proposal, he would then employ an architect, obtain licences and permits, and divide ownership of each individual garden and plot. These would then need to be registered on the deeds of all six properties.

'If only one person refuses, then it will not happen.'

Being a glass-half-empty kind of person, Francisco put forward this proposal in a very pessimistic and negative way but it was a glimmer of hope and he wouldn't be doing his job if he hadn't told us. We had to be optimistic. Surely it was to everyone's advantage to own their personal plot of land but we were concerned that the cost of all of this work would put it out of reach again. We couldn't afford a hefty legal bill.

Adrian and I looked at each other and spoke simultaneously. 'How much will all this cost?'

Francisco's eyes widened. 'No, not you. The Richardsons will pay. This is their responsibility. You will not purchase unless they agree to these terms.'

It's an odd thing in Spain that a solicitor can, and often does, work for both parties in any transaction. They're not concerned with conflict of interest. In our case Francisco was working for both the vendor and the purchaser and he was determined to do what was right. This strange arrangement was working to our advantage.

We didn't have to wait long to hear from Francisco. Fortunately the deeds named the neighbours on all sides of the property so there was no major detective work needed to track them down. All parties readily agreed to the division of land and Francisco wasted no time in appointing an architect who confirmed the local council were also in agreement. From that point onwards, the purchase went ahead without a hitch. It was confirmed that our money was already in Spain from the sale of the El Nacarino house and that money would be withheld from that to pay the cost of the separation of the gardens. The additional work hadn't caused any great delay and we were still able to complete in three months.

Four years later the properties still haven't been properly divided up. After a year of slowly moving Spanish bureaucracy, the person dealing with it went off sick and, as far as we know, hasn't yet returned to work. Something has happened though because now, instead of our address just being a plot number, we have street names. There are fresh new signs on every corner telling us where we are.

Finalising the sale wasn't the end of our dealings with Francisco. After-sale problems with the sale of El Nacarino rumbled on for over a year and caused a lot of worry for the new owner and us. Despite the paperwork being in order, the house completely legal, and the sale being trouble free, at some point someone in the town hall in El Nacarino decided the house wasn't properly registered. It was legal when we bought it and, at every point in the renovation, the proper licences had been obtained and the registration updated but we found ourselves in the bizarre situation of having allegations levelled at us that we'd sold an illegal property.

The ground floor was legal, the staircase was legal, the

roof terrace was legal but the floor in between had been dropped off the registration and was therefore, somehow, an illegal build. The original house had been built with two floors and had stood that way for 60 years but there was no budging the council. At one point we were told they wouldn't register the house in the name of the new owner and we should give him his money back. It was even suggested we may have to knock down the middle floor. No amount of paperwork was going to satisfy the zealot at the council. Even Francisco was thinking it had become a face-saving exercise. Someone had made a mistake and was not going to back down.

One day I received a telephone call from Francisco asking me to come and see him. 'Bring your husband. This is the only way it is going to get settled.'

The 'bring your husband' bit related to a frustratingly idiotic, archaic, patriarchal, mindset that decided that the latest bit of illegality was that I had sold the house, which was solely registered in my name, without my husband's consent. I needed to go with him to the notary's office where he could say 'I do' all over again and give his permission for me to sell *my* property. Any hope of equality and female emancipation died a death that day along with my independence and sense of free will. Franco is alive and well and survives in the strongly beating heart of a jobsworth at El Nacarino town hall.

I grudgingly trailed along behind Adrian and Francisco to the notary's office where, to his credit, Adrian said I didn't need his permission; the property was mine to do as I wanted with.

'Does that mean yes?'

'Of course.'

Job done. Face saved.

Our first night in our new house, we slept on mattresses on the floor, surrounded by boxes. Caz and Austin had been waiting for us when we arrived the previous evening, had switched on the outside lights, and as a welcome had left the gates open wide. As we climbed out of the car, the warmth of the evening enveloped us, the lights illuminated the flowers and the trees that stood still in the calm unmoving air. It was perfect. A magical moment.

Inside, our belongings that had been transported from Austin's were waiting for us, ready for boxes to be opened and sorted, and the house felt as happy and welcoming as it did when we first came to view. This was a good move. After Caz and Austin left, we sat outside for a while, opened a bottle of wine, and then fell onto the mattresses to sleep. The boxes could wait until tomorrow.

Next morning I woke early. We'd arrived very late the evening before but the excitement of being in our new home was too much. I wanted to get out there and touch it, see it, feel it. The novelty of walking straight out of my front door into a secluded and beautiful garden was too exciting for me to be able to sleep and I couldn't wait to get out there.

In the stillness of the early morning, the air was clean and clear; everything looked brighter and, as I opened the door and looked out, I was met by a riot of colour. The vibrant blue of the sky was the perfect backdrop for the dazzling, brilliant white of the buildings and the sparkling water in the pool. A few oranges still clung tenaciously to branches, defying the season, their warm glow contrasting delightfully with the glossy green leaves of the trees. Red, pink, and white oleanders dotted the garden, exquisite but lethally poisonous; purple convolvulus clung to the fence; and, all around, the sharply sweet-smelling orange, red, and yellow of the lantana, the Spanish flag shrub, lined the paths. Here and there a cock crowed and, right in front of me, a pretty hoopoe bird with its headdress and black and white stripy wings hooped its way into flight.

As the sun had already risen, it was warm and destined to get hotter as the day wore on. I took my morning coffee over to the pool and, sitting in the sunshine with my feet in the water, looking at these idyllic surroundings, life couldn't have felt better.

The journey that had brought us here had had a few bumps but, apart from those hiccups, it had been a smooth and pleasant ride. I'd loved El Nacarino, albeit we were there longer than we'd initially intended, and was glad of the time we spent there. I was sad to leave and would miss my kind and generous neighbours, especially Concha, but, in the time we'd been there, I'd developed health problems and the hills were too much for me. I wasn't going to miss those. Some days I couldn't make it up to the roof terrace and, during a bad spell, I was a prisoner on the ground floor and, if we wanted to go out, it needed to be a car ride.

Adrian was happy to leave. A country boy at heart, he couldn't understand the attraction of going on holiday to a little townhouse where the only outside space was viewed through houses from the roof terrace. He had no regrets. We were moving somewhere better where the quality of life for us would massively improve; somewhere we would get everything we'd wanted for such a long time.

I was going to miss so much in El Nacarino. My quirky little house, the whoosh of the church bells that swept through the house when the bells rang, the friendship and companionship, the feeling of never being alone, the general bustle of the town, but we had good things ahead of us. We had successfully moved to pastures new. Right at that moment though, I was happy to be where I was, enjoying my coffee beside our pool.

A priority was going to be furniture. We had a bistro set, coffee tables, and a single bed. Adrian had a greater priority which was to splash around in the pool, simply because he could. A few days later, we steeled our nerves for a drive on the ring road around Seville and braved a trip to IKEA for sofas and chairs then the day after that a trip to Écija, a nearby town, for beds. By the time we went back to the UK, the house was well equipped and comfortable. It had stopped being just a house. It looked and felt like a home and the pool had been well and truly used.

Learning the Lingo

With my father coming from the Gorbals in Glasgow, I'd grown up feeling bi-lingual. As a child I got used to acting as interpreter and explaining to my friends how cuddy means pony, puddocks are tadpoles, oxters are armpits, a jelly piece is a jam sandwich, and, if he offers you a poke, don't panic; he's asking if you want an ice cream. Oh yes, I was fluent in both English and Jockanese so how much more difficult would it be to learn Spanish, I'd thought, before we initially bought a house in Spain?

Armed with my BBC *Get by in Spanish* tapes and a Spanish 'O' level, I was prepared and confident. I could work on this and what I didn't know would fall into place. But I'd spent five years learning standard Castillian Spanish and then we'd bought our first house in El Nacarino, Andalusia.

Andalúz. A language where the letters S and D are rarely pronounced, where the ends of words run indecipherably into the next, and where colloquialisms are completely different. I had never felt more lost or inadequate than when we first arrived in Spain.

I have no idea why I hadn't thought this through. If a

person learns Oxford English, they're going to struggle in Glasgow, Liverpool, or Birmingham and I should have known better than most how this would work. No Spanish teacher had ever said to me, 'I am teaching you the language but you won't understand a word when you get there,' but that's exactly what happened. It got better over time but, when we left El Nacarino eight years later, I was still more or less completely baffled. I could make myself understood but heaven help me if anyone spoke back.

In a town where letters are lost, I never did get to grips with hearing and translating at the same time. I understood that words like *complicado* (complicated) would become *complicao*, that *cantado* (sung) would be *cantao* but, in rapid-fire Spanish, they didn't instantly or easily compute and it was always some time later that the penny dropped, too late to give a sensible response or any slight semblance of intelligence or understanding. I was always at least ten minutes behind the conversation, struggling to keep up and missing large chunks altogether.

A request to speak slowly was met with an understanding, and sometimes sympathetic, smile and the conversation would start again slowly and then gradually build up to the same rapid pace. I spent a lot of time smiling and nodding but getting completely lost, still trying to process the previous conversation. A conversation with Concha usually ended with us both in a bewildered hug, laughing at each other's lack of comprehension.

There was a lovely incident with Findley, who was learning Spanish at school in England. As Paco was leaving one day, Findley went to say goodbye. Tickled with delight, Paco excitedly exclaimed in his limited English, 'Ahhh, he speak Spanee!' And there you have it. Andalúz English. The important thing is to try.

There are some people, my husband being one of them,

who struggle with learning a new language. Try as he might, Adrian can't get to grips with the new words. He does work hard at it, bless him, but it just doesn't happen. He remembers words to be polite, a lot of words in fact, but he doesn't have the confidence to try a whole sentence. You wouldn't know it to see him deep in conversation with our gardener; on common ground the words don't seem to be important. We have, appallingly, heard of people in our inland community who genuinely believe the Spanish should learn English to accommodate us and think it's OK to go into a restaurant and order fish and chipio. There is scorn when they aren't understood. It's no wonder we Brits have a reputation for being lazy with languages.

My disasters with the language paled beside John and Shirley who had no knowledge of even the basics. I lost count of the times I had to explain that the *muebles* factories made furniture and didn't churn out marbles, and that the *bomberos* were firemen, not the bomb squad. I gave up at the *cementerio*. As much as Adrian struggles with the language, even he wouldn't go there for a bag of ready-mix.

One day we were loading up the car to go home and Concha, as was usual, came out to say goodbye. Hugs, kisses, a confirmation of when we would be back, and, '*Bo-vee-aye.*'

'*Bo-vee-aye?*'

'*Sí, bo-vee-aye.*' This time with a hand waved above her head which I interpreted as an aeroplane.

'*Oh, sí. Vamos al aeropuerto. Hasta la próxima vez. Adiós.*' Oh, yes. We're going to the airport. See you next time. Goodbye.

'*Bo-vee-aye.*' There it was again. We drove away clueless and were halfway to Malaga before I realised that *bo-vee-aye* was *buen viaje* — have a safe journey.

As we were leaving El Nacarino, Carmen, our neighbour and manager of the corner shop, asked where we were going.

'To Acerico,' I said.

'Acerico? Oh no. They have a funny accent there. You will never understand anybody.'

Just 40 minutes down the road from El Nacarino, Acerico is hardly another country, however the attitudes and ethos are completely different and, as Carmen said, the accent is different. I understand and I am understood. It is rare to come across pure Andalúz here. The exception to this is Pedro, the plumber.

I hadn't met Pedro before the day I was obliged to wait for him outside the local restaurant beside the main road to direct him to our new house. He pootled up in the obligatory white van which, in Spain, is a cross between the family car and a workhorse. Even without the vehicle, I would have recognised him. A friend I'd recently made had arranged the meeting. 'You can't miss Pedro. He looks like a plumber.'

So there I was one morning in the busy car park of the restaurant, watching workers pull up and go in for breakfast. Any one of them could have been Pedro but then I saw the white van bouncing up the slope towards me, an arm furiously waving out of the window. Elaine was right. There was no mistaking Pedro. He tumbled out of the car unshaven, his leathery face split ear to ear with the biggest and warmest smile, dressed in what I can only describe, with shame, as peasant clothes — straw hat, baggy trousers, and a loose shirt that had seen better days. Pedro was not only a plumber, he was a happy plumber. And the one and only Andalúz speaker I'd met since we'd moved to Acerico. And I was about to take him home and talk technical. This was going to be fun.

I drove in front of Pedro back to our house, zig-zagging to avoid the dozens of potholes en route, Pedro bouncing along behind me in his white van, still grinning. We pulled into our driveway only for Pedro to tell me he'd just come from the house on the corner. At least I think that's what he said. We'd just driven five miles for him to come back to his starting point.

We'd engaged Pedro to connect a dishwasher. What we hadn't conveyed to him was there was no plumbing ready to connect to and he would need to install it. The next half an hour was a confusing and incomprehensible jumble of words, mime, and diagrams, Pedro good-naturedly smiling his way through it and laughing at my bewilderment. I like to think he thought it was the plumbing that was confusing me as he didn't stop talking, so clearly didn't see language as a problem. He understood me OK; this lack of comprehension was mine, not his.

As Pedro wasn't expecting to carry out a complete installation, he'd come unprepared and needed to leave to buy the parts necessary to complete the work. He'd spent some time under the sink in wide-eyed amazement, sucking in air through his teeth at yet another Heath Robinson-type English DIY job. Much was going to be needed before this dishwasher was going to be usable. I spent a lot of time smiling and saying, '*Sí, claro,*' even though I had no idea what he was saying. 'Of course,' seemed the only appropriate reply to make.

Pedro told me he would phone me to let me know when he was coming back. I felt the blood drain.

'No!' Not the telephone! Deep breath, calm... aaaand smile. 'Not the telephone please, Pedro. A text would be better.'

'*Claro,*' and he was off, smiling and waving his way down the road.

Despite the peasant disguise and the thick Andalúz accent, Pedro is educated and very literate. From then on we communicated extremely well by text. The next time he came, he brought a notebook and pen.

There are a lot of pitfalls in the Spanish language. A mistake can lead to howls of laughter or shock and horror on the face of the person you're talking to. I remember the mortified look on my gardener's face when I told her I'd pooed myself instead of saying I was scared of next door's dog. *Miedo* and *mierda* are awfully similar when you're struggling for words. One says 'I have fear' while the other says 'I have done something very embarrassing and anti-social.' Incontinence isn't a laughing matter in any language and *mierda* is considered a bad word in Spanish. These are things that aren't on the syllabus when a foreign language is taught. They ought to be. In the interest of furthering education, I will give out a few pointers.

In a restaurant, an order of *pollo* and chips will get you chicken. *Polla* and chips will get you raised eyebrows; you'll have just ordered male genitalia.

When buying furniture, it's as well to remember that *cajones* are drawers while *cojones* are balls, again of the genitalia variety. My friend Debbie made this mistake in IKEA when she was buying a wardrobe.

Also, tildes (the squiggle above the letter n) and accents can be crucial. Be careful and don't leave them off!

Mi papá tiene 47 años. My father is 47 years old.

Mi papa tiene 47 anos. My potato has 47 anuses.

You get the picture.

One evening, Rafa and Dolores, our new Spanish friends in Acerico, had come to spend a few hours with us. We were having a few drinks and laughs and then Dolores asked me where my father-in-law was. Brian was staying with us at the time but was nowhere to be seen. He's an avid birdwatcher and was excited to find we had a nightjar living in our garden, a relatively rare and elusive bird. In the evening he would disappear into the darkness of the garden and wait patiently for hours in the hope of getting a photograph of it, his location only given away by the frequent flashes from his camera.

'*Está en el jardín buscando pajeros*,' I told Dolores.

From her position on the edge of the pool, Dolores didn't move. Her head stayed resolutely facing the floor; only her eyes moved as they swivelled towards me.

'*Pájaro.*'

'*¿Pájaro?*' I queried, strongly emphasising the first 'a' as she had done.

'*Sí.*'

The raised eyebrows and her quiet but firm mode of speech told me I'd gaffed again and this was more than just a mispronunciation. After Dolores and Rafa left, I looked it up in my colloquial-Spanish dictionary and discovered I'd just told her my father-in-law was down the garden watching wankers.

The good thing about making a mistake with language is it's an excellent way to learn. Embarrassment is a good reminder and, once you've ordered a wardrobe with testicles, you aren't likely to make the same mistake again.

It works the other way round too. Until recently there were so few Brits in our area that a restaurant menu would always be in Spanish. As more and more foreigners have moved in, there have been attempts at translating and adding an English version. One restaurant close to us was proudly advertising *huevos revueltos de la abuela* (grandmother's scrambled eggs), temptingly translated into English as grandmother's revolting eggs.

It's also wise to be careful about throwing any other

language into the mix. Spanglish is just about acceptable and most Spanish people are so pleased if you attempt to speak the language. However, I remember an early trip to Barcelona where it didn't pan out so well. I stopped to ask directions from an elderly gentleman. I completely forgot the Spanish word for station (*estación*) and confused it with the French word, *gare*. With my dodgy pronunciation, it came out as *guerra* so I'd just pounced on this unsuspecting old man and asked him the way to the war. I had no idea someone that age could move so fast. It was impressive.

Rafa and Dolores

After being ripped off so badly in El Nacarino, we were a lot more cautious in the new house, particularly as we had a timely reminder of our mistakes shortly after we moved to Acerico. I received a surprise call from Sandra, the ex-friend who'd been secretly renting out our house in El Nacarino. In her role of B&B landlady, she often had people staying with her who were looking for property in the area and so, at some point, I'd told her that, if at any time she were to show any of her guests around and it led to them buying the house, I would pay her the commission I would have paid the estate agent. It was a genuine offer and I'd made it some years previously. To my knowledge she never took a single person to view and, when we did eventually sell, it was through an estate agent. Sandra was phoning to ask for the money I had promised her when the house sold.

With 3,000 sq ft of garden at our new house, we needed someone to come in while we were away otherwise we would be coming back to a wilderness. This time we went to a tried and trusted friend, Austin, and employed the same two people who worked in his home. This time we haven't been disappointed.

Rafa and Dolores come every ten days, more or less. It isn't enough for a garden of our size but they treat it as if it's their own and it's kept immaculate. The problem with this is we feel we need to ask them first before we do anything. We uncovered some old gravel paths that were badly overgrown and so we spent a week clearing away plants and shrubs and then re-laid them with fresh gravel. They looked really smart and had made some parts of the garden much more accessible. We liked it a lot. Rafa, on the other hand, was concerned, needing to check on what we'd done, how we'd done it, consternation written all over his round face. We got the strong impression we were in trouble because we hadn't asked permission.

Rafa and Dolores are the kindest, most amiable people on the planet; both fairly short, both fairly round, tanned chestnut from working out in the sun every day, and they adore each other. She calls him Nené (baby). He drops off the 's' on the end of her name and calls her Dolorey. They look after each other and us. We love them.

Last summer there was a palm beetle infecting palm trees across Andalusia and hundreds of palms died. A friend lost a beautiful, magnificent tree due to this infestation. Once they get a hold, there's little that can be done to save a tree. Rafa was concerned and looking extremely worried.

'Jean, *hay un gran problema. Tienes picudo rojo.*' Jean, there is a big problem. You have a red weevil.

My big, beautiful palm had been attacked. While Rafa looked the tree up and down, he was telling me what he thought could be done to save it. He was going to give it an injection. As he was talking, his arm shot up in the air and caught a bug mid-flight, the red palm weevil, a nasty little beastie intent on destroying my symbol of paradise. Rafa showed it to me, holding it between his thumb and forefinger, and ripped its ugly head off. Palmageddon had begun.

The rest of the morning was spent inspecting the tree and spraying it with insecticide. Rafa took a brown plastic bottle with a milky fluid and stuck into the side of the tree. This was the injection and, over the next few weeks, the palm sucked up the liquid that killed the bugs and restored it to health. Rafa tenderly nursed and nurtured that palm as if it was his own child. There is surely not a tree in the whole of Spain that ever had better care. It thrived and he was rewarded for his efforts this year by seeing it flower for the first time. As if joyous to be alive, clusters of tiny, white, star-shaped flowers hung in gratitude below broad, fan-shaped, spiky leaves; its gift to Rafa for saving its life.

(I confess that, until I saw the beetle gripped by Rafa, I'd been rescuing them when they fell in the swimming pool. I thought they were harmless bugs. It's my guilty secret. I haven't dared tell Rafa and you must promise me you won't either.)

There was a bare spot in the garden that I wanted to fill and I decided a persimmon tree would be perfect. The type I had in mind is hardy, doesn't grow too big, and would be very different from everything else we already had. This was carefully researched and deemed to be Roberts-proof. The trees are apparently really easy to take care of, disease and pest free, drought tolerant, and long living. We read the requirements:

1. Light, well-drained, sandy soil. Check.

2. Open, sunny spot, sheltered from winds. Check.

3. Weed-free environment. Check.

4. Plenty of compost or rotted manure. Check.

No problem. Plus we would get Rafa to plant it for us. What could go wrong?

Now Rafa takes these things seriously. Having got over my

clumsiness in asking him to buy me a tree instead of telling him I was going to buy one, he and Dolores decided they would buy one for us and take responsibility for its health and well-being. All we would need to do was water it. Simple.

We had to wait for the right time of year but eventually the tree arrived. Excitedly, Rafa and Dolores took us to see it, faces wreathed in smiles, very pleased with their gift. It was, indeed, lovely; about 4ft tall, sturdy and healthy. They gave us strict instructions on how to care for it. It would need four buckets of water every three days. Not three, not five, but four buckets. Fingers were waved in front of us to emphasise and, in case we hadn't understood, this was repeated several times. We'd been left something precious and we needed to care for it like a baby and not be negligent parents.

As they were leaving that morning, Rafa called out, '*Recuerde, cuatro cubos.*' Remember, four buckets. From that moment on, it was called the four-bucket tree.

We looked after that tree. I promise we did. It had its four buckets every three days; we kept it weed-free; we mulched it to keep in the moisture and keep the roots cool in summer. It died anyway.

I watched, my heart heavy with guilt, as Rafa stood forlornly looking at our disaster.

'*¿Regaste?*' he asked. Did you water it?

'Yes, just as you told us.'

'*¿Cuatro cubos?*'

'Yes.'

A shake of the head and a funny clicking noise in the back of his mouth showed his disappointment. He was puzzled and saddened. What could have gone wrong? It was as if this was a personal failure. He was visibly upset. And then this gentle man was consoling us on our loss.

'*Os compraremos otro. El próximo será mejor; será fuerte.*' We will get you another. The next one will be better; it will be strong.

This time Rafa's brother would choose us a good one and Rafa would plant it with special care.

We killed that one too.

It's comical to see Rafa and Adrian deep in conversation, neither one of them speaking a word of the other's language but understanding each other perfectly. Lots of hand signals and laughter but cars, pumps, pools all get chewed over, the workings dissected, and the world put to rights. Man talk.

The day the pool pump died and I had no water to top it up, I was in Spain alone. Adrian was back in the UK. It was at a time when the pool was leaking badly and needed to be topped up daily but we had town water for drinking so I wasn't without. I sent a message to Dolores to let them know and to say when they were next over perhaps Rafa could look at it. It wasn't urgent. They weren't due for another week but that evening, just as it was getting dark, the gate opened and there they were. They'd finished a full day's work and driven an hour to get to me to help.

The pump was pulled apart, put back together, pulled apart again. Nothing worked. Pipes were inspected, water levels checked, motor functioning gone over with a fine-tooth comb.

They declined all offers of food and drink. They had work to do and, if they could, they were going to make sure I had water that night. As I was only getting in the way and had no useful suggestions to make, I left them to it. I went back about half an hour later just in time to see Rafa's bulky frame disappearing down the well.

They stayed until 11 o'clock and then had another hour to drive home. The pump wasn't fixed but it wasn't for the want of trying. They'd tried every trick in their repertoire. Each time it failed, Rafa would shrug, shake his head, and start all over again. Even with their extensive experience and expertise, they just couldn't bring it back to life. In the end they apologised profusely, as if they'd let me down. I felt so guilty. These kind-hearted, hardworking people were leaving for home, which they would probably reach around midnight, and they would be up working in someone else's garden by 7:30 the next morning yet here they were apologising to me.

The following morning I had a message from Dolores. She'd been up early and spoken to Felipe, the plumber in her village, who would be round later that day.

Rafa and Dolores are joined at the hip. You get one, you get the other. Rafa doesn't drive so Dolores is his transport. She is also his rock. Theirs is a real, solid partnership and to see them together is lovely. They are happy, content, and completely comfortable with each other. They have two adored children whom Dolores refers to as the king and queen of her home. They aren't rich financially but they have something that money can't buy. They have wealth beyond price.

Dolores works alongside Rafa in the garden; she also keeps our pool sparkling. If there's any extra needing doing, then Dolores is our man, or woman. Practical and down to earth, nothing is too much trouble and there seems to be nothing she can't do. She is superwoman! Ceilings needing painting? Yep, that's one for Dolores. Pool needs a scrub? She's on it. Want the world's best olives? Go to Dolores; she's ace. When Austin's huge house needed painting, guess who did it? Right again. Dolores. No, not just the inside; all of it — walls, masonry, pool, everything. All by herself. Rafa does trees.

There's a slight tinge of Andalúz with Rafa. Not too much and I don't have difficulty understanding him. He has infinite patience with me and, because of his good nature, conversation is easy. Dolores is well spoken and I learn a lot from her. There's no embarrassment or inhibitions about correcting me when I so often say something wrong and it helps me no end. Since I swore at her by accident, she's not taking any chances and my Spanish has come on in leaps and bounds. She knows I need help. She also steps in and corrects me when she sees me doing something cock-eyed. There's a Spanish way of doing things and a wrong way. I learn from experts.

Acerico

It gets hot in Acerico; blowing-up-the-digital-screen hot. By the time it gets to 50 on the thermometer, the screen is black. The area around us is known as the frying pan of Spain with Écija having the highest recorded temperatures of anywhere in the country. We should have kept this in mind when we were buying garden furniture.

Our family were on their way over and we only had two chairs. There were a few wooden benches dotted around our garden but we needed seating where we could all be together. The quickest and cheapest option was plastic garden chairs. Until that point there'd been more pressing purchases and so we'd just made do. This now got upgraded to a priority. A quick trip into town and we soon had ten inelegant, but practical, shiny new chairs and a couple of loungers, all ready in time for our guests. By the time the family arrived, everywhere looked inviting and neat and there was more than enough seating for the comfort of everyone.

The first sign these chairs weren't fit for purpose was a few days after they arrived. We were all sitting around the pool and Adrian was telling a story. He tends to use his hands when he speaks and, right then, he was windmilling away, emphasising a particularly funny point, bouncing about a bit at the same time. I watched with horror as he slowly slid towards the floor, the legs on the chair melting underneath him. He was quickly, or I should say slowly, followed by my son-in-law Michael. One by one, the legs buckled. These chairs were giving out in the heat of the sun.

Thank goodness my family have a sense of humour and I have a very inventive husband. The following day Adrian disappeared into the shed with ten chairs and came out again with five. He'd doubled them up and bolted the legs together, giving us five very sturdy (and ultimately expensive) plastic chairs. They worked a treat, but for shade only. No one was going to risk sitting on them in the sun.

The rest of the summer was wonderful. We were happy with our lovely new home with its beautiful garden and we had a constant stream of visitors. It was a summer of fun, mostly centred around the pool, the privacy and space giving us all a wonderful sense of freedom. The sun shone continuously. We played games, had pool races, or lazed on swings or in hammocks; no rules, just everybody having a good time. I watched, heart in mouth, as Suzanne back-flipped into the pool, and then spellbound as Eva glided below the surface, long hair floating out behind her, an adorable water nymph. The boys played the game of seeing who could hold their breath underwater the longest, turning on their biggest smiles as they broke the surface again. Clearly not concerned with oxygen starvation to the brain, Christian was the all-out winner with almost three minutes.

Several years later and we have new neighbours from Denmark.

I know this from their car number plate. Laughter comes from the garden and we hear the sound of splashing in the pool. In the still air of the evening, the sound of corks popping and happy chatter floats across the garden from their direction. They sound a jolly bunch but they aren't very sociable. A wave in passing is ignored as is a cheery *hola* outside in the narrow street. In our one-car-wide lane, a vehicle must wait or pull to one side to let another pass. They take no prisoners so we invariably wait for them and they breeze past or turn into their gateway without making eye contact. Their unfriendliness borders on ignorance which I find so strange and unexpected in this country where the opposite is the norm. I don't mind that they're unfriendly. I mind that they are rude. Just sayin'.

Throughout the year our bountiful garden keeps us supplied with fruit — figs, plums, pomegranates, grapes, lemons, and, of course, oranges. January is the time when we're rewarded for all those hours of watering trees and drinking margaritas throughout the year. It's orange harvest time. Big, fat, sweet, juicy oranges. Tons of them. With 50 trees there's an enormous amount and we become very popular with our friends and neighbours at this time of year. We have one tangerine tree, which I guard jealously, and one marmalade-orange tree; the rest are deliciously, mouth-wateringly awesome. There's nothing like waking up to freshly squeezed juice made from your own oranges, hand-picked that morning. It's a wonderful way to live.

Orange trees are very satisfying all year round. They're evergreen so perpetually beautiful and in April the heady scent of their blossom fills the air. Orange blossom, the symbol of love and romance. The smell is intoxicating and at night time seems to intensify. Walking into the orange grove on a warm evening with the giddy smell of orange blossom and the sound of cicadas is heavenly. The blossom itself is pretty but the white flowers are so tiny it's hard to believe they can pack such a punch.

There are times in the year when there are fruit and flowers on the tree at the same time and, as the fruits ripen, the bright orange orbs against the dark green backdrop make a stunning display. I hope the novelty of sitting on a bench and just reaching up and plucking a fruit straight off the tree never fades. It's a magical feeling.

One grumpy neighbour aside, it feels as if we pretty much have everything. We close the gates and we are happy, content to be here with no real desire to leave. One day that may happen but, for now, I am in love. I am in love with this country and I am in love with my life. This is our happy place.

Mum, the Toilet's Leaking

When we bought the house, it looked immaculate. The previous owners were house-proud and everything was pristine. When we moved in, we found everything had been left in impeccable order. There was nothing for us to do. If we'd had furniture, we could have simply put it in place and just carried on. My only concern was my ability to keep it to its existing standard. I had big shoes to fill in that respect. The only things not to our liking were the lime green walls in the living room. Everything else seemed perfect.

Not long after we moved in, the kitchen worktop began to sag in one corner. There was a clear gap between sealant and tiles that we initially thought may have been caused by the ants which are a continual problem in this part of Spain and need constant monitoring. We'd seen ants coming up through there and had zapped them with powder. Now it looked as if they were causing considerable damage.

At the same time, we were having problems with electricity arcing between two closely placed plug sockets; a dangerous situation and I'd already received a couple of mild shocks. Apart from the inconvenience of being frequently plunged into darkness, there was a very real risk of fire. They needed attention and quickly.

When we removed the sockets, there was a Heath Robinson arrangement of wires and cables behind, minus any sign of earth or insulation. It's a myth that Spanish electricity has no earth. I've heard this said many, many times but it simply isn't true. It's just not earthed in the same way as in the UK. This wiring had clearly been done by someone who believed the legend and any earthing was non-existent. How nobody had been killed in that kitchen is beyond me.

Removing the sockets and making safe the wiring should have been an afternoon's work, a simple job. Two separate and spaced sockets, properly wired, were all that was needed to replace the dodgy double socket. This came off easily and, with it, most of the tiles, domino effect, one after the other, each tile with the minutest dab of tiling cement that had been holding it to the wall. A look in the cupboard under where the worktop sagged showed there was no side or back to the cabinet. The top was held up by a skyhook.

This afternoon job of a quick repair took two and a half days of electrical work, carpentry, and tiling. A lot of effort in the heat of summer and eventually it looked just the same as it had before we started. Quite dispiriting to have nothing to show for our exertions but at least we were safe.

That first summer, our daughter Chrystal and son-in-law Charlie were staying in the casita.

'Mum, the toilet's leaking,' Chrystal came to tell me one morning. 'The bathroom floor's wet. Can you or Adrian come and look?'

I hurried over.

'Look, when the toilet's flushed, water bubbles up into the

shower.' She showed me, just in case my nose hadn't spotted the problem. 'It's pretty gross.'

'I'll have to phone Austin,' I told her. 'The casita isn't on mains drainage so all waste drains into a cesspit. If it's coming back up, it's a serious problem.'

The risk of our guests paddling in effluent was very real. A cesspit is a very simple arrangement where everything drains away into a hole in the ground. Eventually it all breaks down and seeps away into the soil. Cesspits rarely need emptying and are a very effective means of sanitation commonly found in country houses all over Spain. We'd recently put in a washing machine and, with the additional water, our cesspit just wasn't man enough for the job, or the jobbies!

Re-routing the washing machine outlet would be easy enough but more pressing was the need to empty the cesspit and we didn't know where it was. We phoned Austin, who phoned Paco, who turned up that afternoon, located the cesspit, and promptly emptied it into our hedge.

During our first summer, we noticed the water in the pool needed to be topped up more often than we expected. Being complete novices with swimming pools, we had no idea if this was due to evaporation or something more sinister. It wasn't much but it was enough to cause concern. We asked Paco have a look at it and he spotted a crack in one of the capping stones he suggested we keep an eye on. He believed it would close up again when the weather cooled down.

'It's normal. It's Andalusia.'

He also said that water sometimes has a way of sealing the problem itself but we should watch what was happening and get back to him if necessary. Paco was right and, as summer came to a close, the water loss became negligible and the following year presented no problem at all. All the family were there together and we were able to enjoy the pool and the sunshine.

The next year, however, the capping stone opened up again and, with it, a crack in the pool itself. Now we were losing five inches of water a day. Emptying a swimming pool in summer isn't to be recommended for all sorts of reasons, not the least being that it could cause more problems than it mends. It should only be done in an absolute emergency so we were advised to get some underwater sealant to make a temporary repair to hold it until any other necessary work could be done later. We bought the sealant but, when trying to use it, it became obvious that a previous repair had already been attempted. By this time the crack had spread from the top to the bottom of the pool. It was looking serious.

One day I was swimming and I noticed a large crack appear at the other end of the pool, opposite the first one. We called Paco back in. One look and the shock on his face was obvious. The pool was about to break its back and, summer or not, needed to be emptied quickly.

Over the next day and a half, the water was drained out into our well. When it was empty, the extent of the damage was clear. It was also obvious it had been a long-standing problem and the previously attempted repair had been useless. The crack had been plugged with window putty. Paco inspected the inside of the pool in disbelief, eyes wide as saucers, looking incredulous.

The repairs took two weeks and Paco and his son Antonio beavered away in the blistering heat of August in the hottest recorded summer for 64 years. Both ends of the pool needed to be stapled to prevent any further problem. They removed the old ladder and built some swanky new steps in its place.

When we bought the house, we were told the pool had been re-painted. What the previous owner forgot to tell Austin was that he'd painted it with ordinary household paint. It took Antonio and Paco a whole day to remove it before the men could come to reline it with fibreglass. In

Andalusia, August is holiday time. Everything shuts down so it wasn't possible to get the fibreglass locally. Eventually Paco found somewhere in Badajoz, another province some distance away, which would deliver, and located workers in a town 40 minutes away who would come and spray it on. They weren't happy to arrive at 6 a.m. only to find they couldn't start work because the house paint needed to be removed.

The result was beautiful. Paco, as usual, did an excellent job. The morning he left, we had an empty, but stunning, lovely new pool with a fifteen-year guarantee of leak-free use. We just had to wait for the paint to dry.

That afternoon Chrystal, Charlie, and Findley surprised us with a visit. It was going to be a good summer.

Another teething problem we had was hot water. On one occasion when we arrived at the end of December, we found the gas water heater was kaput. There was a very expensive, computerised, gas-fired boiler on the outside of the house that had been working extremely well. We were longing for a hot shower after our long journey, turned on the taps, and… nothing; just an icy stream of very uninviting cold water came out. In El Nacarino we'd had an antiquated heater which never let us down. It blew out occasionally, threatened to blow up often, but we were never without hot water. This new-fangled, top-of-the-range, modern contraption with all its whistles and bells didn't like being left and was throwing a major hissy fit. No amount of coaxing would get it to work and we had guests arriving in a couple of days.

Time for another call to Paco.

In Spain, knowing one person gives you access to a whole village of people. If the person you know can't fix your problem, he will always know someone who can, usually a brother, or cousin, or an uncle. This time it was Felipe, Paco's neighbour and, conveniently, a plumber.

Felipe arrived the next day and declared the gas heater dead. Try as he might, he couldn't bring it back to life again. It hadn't liked being left for a couple of months and just couldn't be economically repaired. Felipe told us that, to continue working effectively, the new gas heaters needed to be in continuous use, something not possible for us in our part-time, expat status. We followed Felipe's advice and had him install an enormous, electric-powered heater and, the following day, we had oodles of hot water, just in time for our friends to arrive. In addition, while he was on site, he serviced our air-con units at no extra cost.

In the main house, there's air-con in three of the rooms. However there was none in the casita. The guests we had the previous summer sweated and sweltered their way through their respective stays. At one point, Michael and Suzanne chose to sleep outside rather than melt away indoors. In the blistering heat of July and August in Seville, fans are just not enough. We decided then to have an air-conditioning unit installed in the casita.

Buying the unit was easy enough. Delivery and fitting were a completely different kettle of fish. The morning of the delivery, we opened our huge double gates wide only to watch the delivery van trundle up along the street and crash straight into them, taking the attached screen with it. Two very grubby men tumbled out, shrugged, shook their heads, and carried the new air-con unit into the casita. Despite getting off to a shaky start, we assumed they knew what they were doing and so left them to it. Half an hour later, they came to tell me the unit was faulty and they would be back the next day with a replacement.

True to their word, they returned the following afternoon with another unit which they attempted to fit and, again, pronounced faulty. This time they didn't remove the faulty appliance but left it fitted to the wall. They looked very sheepish when I pointed out it was skewiff and that they'd left loads of filthy black and greasy handprints all over my white walls. It would take a lot of cleaning. Another shrug, two heads shaking as they promised to return the next day. I hoped they wouldn't.

Bright and early the next morning, the van arrived again, this time with two different installers, both of them squeaky clean and, unlike the other two, articulate and smiling. What a relief! It turned out the appliance wasn't faulty; it had just been installed wrongly and they had it working in no time. Little could be done to straighten it so we decided we would just have to accept it as it was and add it to the list of oddities we had to get used to in Spain.

In any new move, there's always the possibility of teething problems. We've had our fair share of these with hidden light switches, wonky wardrobes, and confusingly labelled fuse boxes. We've had some shocks (literally!) and some surprises, some unexpected expenditures, and an awful lot of work.

We were once asked if we regretted buying the house. Not for a second. Despite some unfortunate mishaps, we've found so much happiness here. This house just keeps on giving and we love it. Every square inch of it. It is home. One day in the future, perhaps I will be Shirley Valentine and I will stay.

Dog Days of Summer

We slipped into the rhythm of life in Acerico very easily with long, hot summer days, sultry nights, and a slow, relaxed, laidback lifestyle. In short, we are chilled whenever we visit.

On a still, summer's evening, we sit under a sky free of light pollution and look up at millions and millions of stars. The Milky Way, shimmering in the black above, and just the two of us down below with wine, good food, and cicadas and bats for company. We sit beside the pool at dusk, watching the swallows swooping and diving, skimming the water for a drink, and we are content; happy here in the peace and tranquillity. I look up into the rash of stars and I see the Big Dipper and Cassiopeia still there and I know all is right with the world. In the still of the morning, with the smell of oranges and lemons hanging in the air, comes the confused cockerel that crows at all hours of the day in a neighbour's garden, close enough to hear, far enough to not be a nuisance, and the sound of donkeys or goats and flamenco music drifting in on the air.

There's a house nearby that, between five and six every evening, plays loud music. You can set your clock by it. It comes on bang on five and goes off dead on six. We call it the party house. Just after five every afternoon, a moped buzzes by on its way to the house. It doesn't stay long before it buzzes off again. Suzanne jokes it's the nightly drug run. The house is scruffy and run-down but, apart from the music and nightly moped, there's no sign that anyone lives there. Besides this, nothing much else disturbs the peace.

We have our own Spanish idyll, our own little bit of paradise. We have hawks gliding overhead and funny little hoopoe birds in the garden. In the evening we hear owls. We rarely see them but we know they're all around us. Lights illuminate the pretty, flower-lined gravel path that winds its way through the garden; fairy lights brighten majestic palm trees; there are numerous cosy nooks in the orange grove and there's our margarita bench where we sit with a cocktail in the evening while Adrian waters the garden. Where I can't garden, I bring light; our garden glitters. We have a lovely, shady paddock with a hammock, and, of course, the pool. At night time we sit under the pergola and watch the sun go down. Heavenly. We no longer have a view as we had in El Nacarino but, here, we have a life.

In this last year, our family has grown by one. Florence arrived. When the last of our three cats in the UK died, we promised ourselves we wouldn't have any more. We travel such a lot and it really wouldn't be fair to them. Besides, the last ones had been a bit of a trial. We'd had Floozie for some time before we adopted two strays, Trigger and Dribbles. Floozie and Trigger hated each other with a passion and they turned our peaceful home into a battleground. Dribbles, being an old lady by then, did her best to stay out of trouble. She just wanted a quiet life. Gentle and loving, a warm lap and a few cuddles were all she asked for. The other two were having none of it and the jealousy between them was vicious. Once Dribbles was removed from laps, they moved on and continued scrapping between themselves.

They fought over meals, who was going through the cat flap first, who was getting the best seat on the sofa, just over being in the same room. I would come home from work and clear up fur from where they'd been fighting and polish out the scratches in the furniture from where Dribbles had climbed higher and higher to get out of the way. Individually, they were adorable. Together, they were an absolute nightmare.

They lived in unhappy disharmony for several years until Floozie was run over and killed right outside our house. Trigger then decided to move out and took himself to live next door, his raison d'être having gone. Poor long-suffering, sweet-natured Dribbles died of old age. When she went we made the conscious decision there would be no more cats. Until Florence decided she needed a home.

We first noticed Florence at dinner one evening when we were back in Acerico. This tiny tortoiseshell kitten had been watching us and, when the meal arrived, brought over a mouse to eat with us. We threw her a few scraps, if for no other reason than to stop the offputting crunching going on down below us, and, from that moment on, she never left us. She slept on a lounger at night and waited outside for us first thing in the morning then followed us around until last thing at night when she would return to her lounger. Wherever we went in the garden, Florence was one step behind us, a cat-shaped shadow. Sometimes she brought her sister with her and we would have a kitten obstacle course to manoeuvre each time we stood up.

Over the next few weeks, with cat-like stealth, they crept their way into our hearts. We were completely smitten. Our neighbour complained to us there were too many cats. Indeed there were dozens of them in his garden, undoubtedly attracted by the plentiful food supply he left for his dogs. Knowing the typical Spanish response to unwanted animals and having watched his dogs playing tug of war with the kittens, we decided the best place for them would be with us. We would take them home.

Florence and her sister were inseparable and it would have been cruel to take one and not the other so it was both or none. We named the sister Carmen and started the ball rolling to get passports for them. Unfortunately, when we began the process, we discovered we needed a minimum of a month for injections and microchips before we could get their pet passports and we only had three weeks left before we headed back to the UK. A pet-carrying company wanted €1,000 for each cat so that was out of the question. Brittany Ferries also had no pet cabins available on our crossing. We'd fallen at the first hurdle.

In the end we very reluctantly decided we would have to leave them behind. They'd survived up until then and we knew they would be OK for food until we got back. They wouldn't starve. They'd shown themselves to be good hunters and our neighbour provided plenty of food for them. He fed his dogs at the weekend and then left them piled up with food until mid-week when he came and fed them again. The only risk was that they might have a tragic accident. All around us is open hunting ground and they could get on the wrong side of some buckshot. The hunters aren't the only ones after the rabbits so dispense with the cats. It was a risk we would need to take. We consoled ourselves with the knowledge that they would go back to our neighbour where they'd come from. He's a kind man but his comment of 'too many cats' was worrying.

We agonised over what would happen. Each time I spoke

with our neighbour, Florence was either weaving her way in and out of my feet or I was cuddling her. He'd also heard me call her by name. Ultimately I believe that's what may have saved her as he believed she belonged to us. Carmen wasn't so lucky.

On the morning we were heading back to the UK, Florence was waiting for us as usual. We left her with cuddles, tears, a ton of food, and a promise from Austin that Rafa and Dolores would keep an eye out for them while we were away. We left, barely able to contain our tears, and drove in silence for the next hour, neither of us able to bring ourselves to speak. We would have broken down. Despite our promises to ourselves that we wouldn't make the kittens too comfortable, we'd fed them, fussed them, and loved them, and couldn't come to terms with leaving them to whatever fate was in store for them.

We were away about eight weeks; an uncomfortable time. Dolores hadn't reported seeing either of them so we had no idea if they were still around. We worried about them all the time.

The evening we arrived back in Acerico, I got out of the car and immediately called for Florence. The following day we both looked for her, calling out for her often. There was nothing — no meowing, no purring, no furry cannonball hurtling towards us; in fact no sign of cats at all. The dozens of kittens had disappeared and our neighbour's comment of 'too many cats' came back to haunt us. Tomcats tend to find homes as mousers but the females don't stand a chance. We weren't optimistic that either Florence or Carmen had survived. It was heartbreaking.

Several days later Rafa and Dolores arrived for their regular visit and, as I opened the door to greet them, a black furry bundle almost knocked me off my feet as it shot past me into the house. Florence! Attracted by Rafa and Dolores' arrival, Florence had found her way back, covered in fleas but healthy, sturdy, and pleased to see us. We fussed her, cried with happiness, and then deflead, dewormed, and fed her.

This was only a short, three-week trip so we were soon back in the same situation we'd been in before where we didn't have time to be able to take her home. But she'd shown she could survive and thrive without us. She was OK. Sadly there was never any sign of Carmen or any of the other kittens and we can only guess what happened to them.

Florence had brought a little gift with her. She was in season. For the next couple of weeks, we protected her honour with vigour, chasing away the clowder of toms that were hanging around our door, howling outside our windows, and dogging her every footstep whenever she went outside. She was only safe outdoors when we accompanied her around the garden, shooing her suitors away. In turn she enjoyed the attention, prowling around like an Aristocat, looking disdainfully down her nose at her ragged bunch of admirers. They would follow her around, sniff where she sat, and line up outside our door like a wistful bunch of moth-eaten carpetbaggers with only one thing on their collective minds.

'We'll have to get her neutered,' I told Adrian eventually. 'We can't take her home but we can ensure her quality of life is better if she's not bogged down by continually producing kittens.'

'OK, let's see if we can get an appointment in the next few days,' he agreed.

The vet in town couldn't see her before we left so, reasoning she wouldn't be in season for long, we agreed to wait until we came back. We were leaving in a few days anyway and, much as she could look after herself, there would be no one to care for her post op. We'd kept her safe; her virtue was still intact.

The night before we left, we went to see Austin in Écija. As we returned to the house in the evening, despite everything we'd done to defend her honour, there was Florence, going at it hammer and tongs behind the casita with the big white tom from next door.

In the countryside in Spain, people keep dogs. Not just one dog but several of all shapes and sizes, their main purpose seemingly being to make a noise and shatter the peace. During our first summer, we were plagued by incessant barking. One dog would start up and eventually there would be a cacophony of barks from all around us.

At the back of us there were two dogs; one a big, russet-coloured, gentle hound and the other an ugly bastard. The russet one was elderly and spent her days sleeping in the shade of a sprawling olive tree. She moved only to slowly turn around, lie down, and go back to sleep again. The other's a white albino. I don't quite know what he is. Bulldog? Pitbull? I haven't a clue but he's an ugly brute and clearly a dangerous breed. He's not a happy dog; squat with a broad chest; big, slobbering, droopy jowls; red, angry eyes; a ferocious bark and a murderous look on him. He's a very frightening dog indeed and for months he terrified me and scared the living daylights out of Dolores. He would see me and launch himself at the chain-link fence with his eyes set on my windpipe. The fence would shake as he landed on it and I would tremble and back off quickly. I've never been quite so scared of any animal as I was of this one and, for a while, I went out of my way to avoid the part of the garden next to his pen.

Our fence is seven feet high and topped with barbed wire so there's no risk of him getting over and, although it's only chain-link, it's sturdy. After weeks of throwing himself at it and failing to get through, he decided to go under and started digging. He'd dug an enormous hole and was almost through by the time we discovered it. We filled our side with bricks, rubble, and heavy pieces of cement, and our neighbour filled his with broken furniture. We were safe for a while.

One day we'd had a BBQ and there was a lot of meat left over. It was mid-week and we hadn't seen our neighbour since the weekend. This wasn't unusual. They're weekenders but pop back in the week to feed the dogs. This week we hadn't seen them. The russet dog had disappeared and only the white one was left. I suggested to Adrian that we throw him the leftovers.

My skin prickled and my heart thudded as I went around the back of the coop to his pen. The reaction was instant. A ferocious bark, a flying leap at the fence, and a snarling, salivating ball of fury, defying me to come closer and promising instant death if I took another step. He wanted blood. Mine. I stood a safe distance away, rooted to the spot, shivering with fear, and threw. Instant silence. The dirt-covered chop lying in the dust didn't stand a chance; it went down his throat without touching the sides.

The change was incredible and immediate. This dangerous killing machine walked to the fence, looked at me, put his head on one side, and lifted his paw, his eyes changing from angry to pleading. He was hungry. I fed him the rest of the meat, backing off slowly when it was gone, expecting him to return to the angry, snarling brute of before but, no, he just quietly watched me walk away. From that day on, he's been my best friend. Who knew it would be that easy?

He's no longer penned up and follows me up and down the garden, from his side of the fence of course. I stand next to him, talk to him, feed him by hand and he's oh so gentle. It's a messy business because he still slobbers but he doesn't attempt to hurt me. I once touched him by accident as I was giving him some food and he went ballistic. This dog has trust issues.

He still hurtles towards the fence when he spots me but now he's pleased to see me; if he had a tail, I'm sure it would wag. For my part, I'm glad the fence is there. I wouldn't like to have clear air between him and me. I still don't trust him. Given half a chance, there's a good probability he would rip my throat out. With a fence between us, I can go out in the garden without fear.

The other upside of this new friendship is that the barking has stopped. Peace and quiet reign. There's a new dog there now. Our neighbour says he's a Spanish Mastin but, to be honest, he looks like an overgrown spaniel. He's *huge* and, by the size of his feet, looks as if he's got a lot more growing to do. He's fun, bouncy, and friendly, and he's been a good influence on my albino friend. He's taken years off him and they play together, their main pastime being a ghastly tug of war with any one of the dozens of stray kittens that live in their garden again. Any unfortunate cat that crosses their path is a potential victim and the game is on. One has the head, the other takes the hindquarters, and they tug and pull. The winner then whips his head round, tossing the kitten away. The kitten gets up, shakes itself down, and trots away. So far no kittens have been harmed in the making of this game (disclaimer for the faint-hearted) but it's very distressing to watch.

Apart from making friends with the local canine population, Adrian and I don't do much. We have a peaceful and happy existence. We've both had enough drama in our professional lives not to look for any more and, hey, we've brought up children. We've had teenagers. What more excitement could we want?

Chicken Summer

One summer we arrived to find chickens in our garden — a mother hen and eleven chicks to be precise. An overload of cuteness. We'd been away a couple of months and, with ours being the only garden around with no dogs, it must have seemed a safe haven. We watched them scrapping around for food, marvelled at how they responded to mum, and found it enchanting when they followed Adrian around as he watered the garden. At night they disappeared and we hoped they would come back.

Next morning there they were again, happily clucking, chirping, and cooing. It was a wonderful sight and, as we pottered around in the sunshine, it felt practically idyllic. They weren't ours; we couldn't keep them but we would enjoy them while they chose to visit. I contacted my friend Kate back in the UK and asked for advice on feeding. I ignored the jokey suggestion of Paxo, along with other, more sensible, suggestions, and gave them Roquefort and grapes for breakfast. From then on they were ours, following our every movement and waiting outside our door for us to come out.

At night we watched as mum flew over the fence and the little'uns filed through the hole they'd dug underneath into the garden of the house owned by the Danes. From there they went into Christoff's garden, our Spanish neighbour, to join his larger flock. I needed to find him and tell him where his birds were lodging.

The first time the mother hen attacked was a bit of a shock but I hadn't recognised it as aggression. It was soon after we arrived and we were sitting at a table outside. She flew up at me. Did she think we had food? Was she begging? She certainly wasn't protecting her chicks. Whatever, it spooked me and I reacted badly.

'Just shoo her away,' Adrian suggested.

'Never going to happen. I'm not reaching out in front of her. That's a step too far for me.'

'What's the problem with birds being close?' he asked. 'You're fine with ducks.'

'I don't know but she scares me. It's like the wretched thing means it.'

For me, it was a quick retreat to the safety of the house but I couldn't stay indoors permanently. Every time I went outside after that, she was there and she flew at me. If she was a short distance away, she would run at me, head down, wings out, neck feathers bristling, scaring the heck out of me. Roadrunner on a bad trip. The air turned blue as this killer chicken attacked me at every turn. Soon I became a prisoner in the house and could only go out with a bodyguard (Adrian) or after the birds had gone home for the night.

One day I'd made it to the compost heap and, as I turned to head back to the house, there my nemesis was in the gateway, defying me to try to get out.

'Adrian!' I called out in panic. 'The chicken won't let me pass.'

All I could hear was laughter in the distance followed by, 'D'you realise how daft that sounds?'

'OK, when you've stopped laughing, d'you think you could just come and rescue me? Please?'

After that I didn't leave the house without a broom or a tea towel to chase her off with but mostly I became too cowardly to step outside when she was around. Yet I still fed the chicks every day, a lot of the time sending Adrian out with food or just throwing it a safe distance away. This bird was seriously stupid, quite literally trying to bite the hand that was feeding her. We named her Doris.

As the chicks grew, they pecked bigger and bigger holes in the garden, dug up plants, and scattered leaves. It became an uphill struggle to stay on top of the mess they were making. Christoff had tried, without success, to reclaim them but wasn't at all bothered to have lost them.

'You should keep them,' he told me one day.

'I can't. They frighten me.'

'Eat them then,' he instructed. 'At least their eggs. *Muy rico*,' he said with a flourish accompanied by pinched fingers to mouth and a lip-smacking noise to indicate what he meant. With a promise of trying again next day, he left. 'Our other neighbour would just put them in the pan,' he declared as we parted company.

Doris continued to terrorise. Hanging out the washing became a survival of the fittest and Adrian was continually on call to stand guard. Doris was making it clear. This was her garden. She was claiming squatter's rights and we had to go. This was war!

One day the Danes arrived with a big dog.

'Adrian, something's up with the chicks tonight,' I said later that evening. 'They were going home but turned and scattered as soon as they approached the fence.'

'Don't worry, they'll be—'

His attempted reassurance was interrupted by loud and ferocious barking from the other side of the fence.

'There's no way they're going through tonight,' I continued. 'That dog's huge.'

We watched as, eventually, the brood regrouped and roosted in an olive tree for the night. Next morning my fear for the chicks resumed.

'Adrian, the chicks are missing.' I hurried indoors to tell him.

'What about Doris?'

'She's distraught. She's calling and looking, calling and looking.'

'Wait a while; maybe they'll be back later.'

Gradually all but two came back that day but Doris was losing chicks and we had to try to get them back home at night to where they would be safer. The problem was that the large dog had moved in for a while. We spent several evenings trying to return the chicks but to no avail. We tempted them with food but, as soon as they got close to the fence, they turned and ran. By then they'd found a permanent roost high in one of our trees.

'It's good they're safe,' I said to Adrian one day. 'But we didn't come to Spain with a plan to keep livestock and we don't want them. We have to do something.'

'And fast,' he agreed. 'If we don't, they'll continue to breed and we'll be overrun with the darned things.'

'OK, so now we have to find a way to get them back to Christoff.'

The problem with chickens is that their behaviour becomes imprinted and, after a couple of days of roosting in our trees, our garden had permanently become home. We hoped that, if we could get them through the fence, they might find it familiar and make their way to their original home.

'Let's enlarge the hole under the fence,' I suggested to Adrian. 'Then we can encourage them back on their route.'

'Maybe it'll work if we wait until the Danes are out and tempt Doris and the chicks with a trail of food,' he agreed.

For nearly two weeks we tried, with varying degrees of success, to get them through. When one or two chicks left, Doris would call them and they'd call back; sometimes she would fly over but it was only to bring them back again. Sometimes the dog would come back and we'd have to abort the mission.

Finally, on one wonderful occasion, after a lot of patience and effort, Adrian managed to grab Doris and push her through. The chicks followed. Lots of contented, happy chicken noises from the other side so we quickly filled in the hole and breathed a sigh of relief. High five!

Then the Danes returned and threw them all back over the fence.

Give us a break! They were only passing through. Let them go where they were meant to be going, I mentally cursed.

Throughout the summer this gestapo hen strutted around the garden, terrorising everyone in her wake. Guests gave her a wide berth, many diving for cover into the pool when she appeared. She was getting worse by the day and had now started to attack Adrian. Occasionally, when she got close enough, she drew blood. She was suffering the hen version of small man syndrome. 'You wanna piece of me? Come on if you think you're hard enough,' she seemed to gloat.

It was becoming obvious that several of the chicks were cocks and were beginning to mimic her behaviour, initially squaring up to each other but how long was it going to be before they started on us? One was bad enough but these little blighters were growing spurs. All previous attempts to repatriate them to Christoff had failed so we needed a different strategy.

'Let's open the double gates,' I suggested one day, 'and leave a trail of food outside in the lane, all the way up to Christoff's house.'

'They're watching us,' Adrian muttered as he gingerly laid food.

'Look, they're following,' I whispered. 'They're falling for it.'

We waited a while longer, making sure they went all the way.

'Now let's close, lock, and padlock the gates. They're safely a long distance away now. We're free!' I punched the air jubilantly.

'It was so easy. How stupid not to think of that before,' Adrian groaned.

'All of them gone and I can walk around without fear.'

The relief was enormous and I was so overwhelmed with emotion that I could have cried.

No more than ten minutes later, Doris flew back over the gate, followed by the chicks. We had chickens squeezing through every bar and orifice, more aggressive than ever.

Then I cried.

All summer they worked their way through the fig trees, the plums, and the pears. Half of our day was spent chasing them out of the big fig tree outside our door. No sooner had we got them out than they were back again. They were relentless. I don't mind sharing but, come on, these birds were stripping everything. Doris always on guard. Machine gun ready.

Adrian is a farm boy. He grew up on a farm in Huntingdon and is used to all kinds of animals. To be fair he wasn't fazed by Doris but he was fed up with her. To him she was just a nuisance. She'd gone for him a few times, drawn blood on occasion, but he'd batted her away and gave back as good as he got. What was happening now though was that he had a wife scared to go out and an aggressive hen and chicks who were eating his crops. If we did nothing, they would never leave; they would breed and we would have dozens of the damn things. Two of them had made their way through the fence back to Christoff but we still had Doris plus seven offspring. We decided to make them feel unwelcome.

'Let's start to chase them,' Adrian suggested in desperation. 'If they have nowhere comfortable to settle then they might move on.'

'Well, they found their way in here by themselves so maybe they can find their way out again to somewhere else,' I said, fingers crossed.

For weeks I never saw Adrian without a long pole in his hand. We didn't want to hurt the chicks but we didn't want them to feel welcome either. The cuteness had long gone. The first time Doris flew at my face it dissipated. She'd already unsettled some summer guests but it was coming towards crunch time. The in-laws were due to arrive, both elderly. My mother-in-law is 93 and walks with a frame. The thought of Doris going on the attack was too horrific to contemplate. And we had grandchildren to consider too.

Before that, our friends Kate and Robert came for a week and Robert, who listens to the *Archers* and is into all things country, had some suggestions to make; some acceptable and some not. In the end we went with not. They keep chickens at home and we thought, in more experienced hands, we would have another go at a kindly removal. Drastic action needed to be taken. It was time for the unthinkable.

In an episode of the *Archers*, poachers had caught pheasants by feeding them with alcohol. Robert mixed whiskey with cereal and waited while Doris and the chicks tucked in. With full tummies they tried to climb the tree. A few steps up, several steps back, but eventually they were all comfortably settled in their roost. A few minutes later, plop, one by one they fell out of the tree, drunk. In the morning they were gone. Only Doris remained. She stayed one more night and disappeared.

A week later my father-in-law saw a genet in the garden...

The Coop

March is our time for DIY. The days have warmed up nicely and aren't too hot so it's a good time to do any outside painting, put a fresh coat of paint around the pool, and trim back hedges in readiness for the summer. From then until May, we potter in the garden, cleaning the soil, replacing light bulbs, and clearing away the pretty wildflowers of spring. It's a nice, unhurried, productive time.

Adrian and I were relaxing one day in March when I received a text from Christian's lovely girlfriend, Georgia:

Did your grandson tell you we're coming over this summer?

It seems like only yesterday the El Nacarino shopkeepers were giving Christian sweets and now he's old enough to bring his girlfriend here, I thought as I typed back:

Yes! It's wonderful. I love nothing more than having my family around me. Can't wait to see you both.

'They'll all be here for the summer,' I told Adrian later,

really excited at the thought of my lovely brood here together. We all live close together in Essex but we don't see each other every day. Here it's different. We each have our own space and privacy but we are all together and I treasure these times.

The planning went into overdrive. Chrystal always lays claim to the casita; Suzanne and Michael would sleep in the house with Eva; Findley would sleep on the daybed in the study and Christian and Georgia would... Just a minute, where would Christian and Georgia go? Two bedrooms in the house and one in the casita wouldn't sleep nine people. We're a close family but we do have boundaries.

Jokingly I said to Adrian, 'They'll have to go in the chicken coop.'

After a lot of head scratching and brain searching, checking out every possible configuration, we realised that it would *have* to be the coop. There was nowhere else.

It finally dawned on Adrian. 'Oh f***.'

Adrian very rarely swears but, over the next few weeks, that expression became a regular part of his vocabulary. He's very good at DIY but he hates it with a passion. However, he loves his family and will do anything to please them. The next month proved he loved Christian very much indeed.

The coop was a fair-sized building that could easily become two rooms; there were already some folding glass doors that divided it up. With a bit of elbow grease and a lot of imagination, they could look rather nice. The trouble was that the rest of it was a shambles and it would be a major undertaking to make it habitable. While there were apertures with bars over them, there were no windows. The brick-built nesting boxes were still cemented in and rendered cement shelves and cubicles reaching to the ceiling lined the walls. The floors were rough cement and the only electricity supply fed a single light bulb. There was no running water or sanitation. And it still smelt of chickens.

Yep, it was going to be a big job.

The following morning saw us in the coop early with the only tool we had — a 1lb claw hammer — knocking out the nesting boxes. With those out of the way, it was surprising how big the floor space was. Easily big enough for a double bed and a couple of small chests of drawers. This could work.

We tapped and hammered away; the piles of rubble grew and, in two days, we'd demolished as much as we needed to see it taking shape. All we had left were two floor-standing, cement cubicles that were perfect for kitchen units and a worktop. Measuring it out, it was clear there was going to be enough room for a bedroom, a kitchen, and a toilet area. Did I mention there was no sanitation? Let's not worry about that. Nothing was insurmountable. In that first couple of days, we became the little engine that could — 'I think I can, I think I can.' We'd started and we weren't going to be beaten. We were going to make this work.

Behind the coop was a compost and general rubbish area, with a whole corner devoted to rubble from the previous owner's projects. In among the debris, we found a huge amount of usable, reclaimed floor tiles. They took a lot of cleaning but were old-fashioned, traditionally Spanish, and rather lovely. They were perfect and, best of all, they were free.

The ceiling of the coop was a single layer of corrugated iron supported by iron beams running the length of the building. These beams were strong but heavily rusted. Adrian abdicated any responsibility for cleaning them and insisted I do it. If I wanted this conversion, I was going to suffer for it as much as he was. Wire brush on metal isn't my favourite sound but I set to with teeth on edge and spent a couple of days brushing and scraping and getting covered in years of muck, mud, and gecko poo. A horrible job but the beams were soon ready for painting. As Adrian had stayed out of the way, he didn't see the bits I skipped. Hammerite covered them beautifully and he still doesn't know. He's the perfectionist, not me.

As Adrian tiled one end, I painted the other. The walls, which had only ever seen one coat of paint, were so porous they needed four coats before they were completely white and stopped smelling of chickens but it was looking cleaner and smelling a lot sweeter. It was, however, taking a long time as I frequently had to stop painting to go and clean the tiles so they could be laid. We needed to work out a different strategy for doing this.

'How about I get up at five and paint 'til ten?' I suggested to Adrian. 'That way I could paint uninterrupted and get a coat on the metal ceiling before the sun comes up and makes it impossible.'

'Bit enthusiastic but if it works for you...'

'Well, then I would clean tiles in the afternoon so you have a steady supply and a clear space to work in.'

That probably clinched the deal. I got to be outside in the sun and Adrian didn't get too grumpy. The work picked up pace.

It's fair to say Adrian wasn't having fun and his patience was tested to the limit. Several hours a day on his knees, doing a job he hated, wasn't good for his temperament and he huffed and puffed his way through. It took almost a week before he was finished but it looked wonderful. A lovely warm, crazed terracotta floor that looked inviting and very Spanish. However much he loathed doing it, he'd done an excellent job.

With the floor and the painting finished, we set about rendering the base units and building a partition wall for the toilet area. OK, maybe not the way round that a professional would do it, but it suited us. It was all taking shape and it was looking good.

We worked throughout March, installing windows, making a kitchen area, and building a base for the toilet. With no running water, it would need to be a Porta Potti. Glamping. Highly fashionable these days.

We asked an electrician friend to look at the electricity and he confirmed it was a strong enough supply to power a lot more lights and appliances so the next week was taken over with installing cables, plug sockets, and switches to run lights, fans, televisions, and a refrigerator.

Water was another matter. The answer was to dig a trench and bury a hose from a standpipe in the garden. This would be well water and would only work when the pump was running. It would be cold water but perfectly OK for washing and cleaning. Drinking water would have to come from a bottle. The wastewater was drained to feed the pomegranate tree at the side.

We worked long hours of hard, physical graft and ended the day exhausted. Quite often the evening meal was a bag of crisps and a bottle of wine. We were too tired for anything else but seeing the work all taking shape was gratifying and rewarding. Christian and Georgia were going to have somewhere very nice to stay and we would have the smartest little henhouse in the whole of Andalusia.

By the time we left at the end of March, the work was more or less complete. Windows were in, curtain poles fitted, a fully functioning electricity supply was installed, and the place had water. The glass-fronted doors had come up a treat. It just needed furnishing and dressing. And Adrian was smiling again. Good humour restored.

We spent April back in the UK and returned to Spain in May to make the finishing touches. There was still some tiling to do but we'd broken the back of it. It was apparent that, although painting the ceiling had helped to make it a little cooler, it was still going to be too hot for comfort inside. The answer was to thatch the roof. We managed to find rolls of rush that were used for fencing and perfect to provide a barrier between sun and tin. A couple of thick layers of that and it was nice and cool inside.

By the time we'd finished the coop, it was beautiful; a complete conversion from dirty home for chickens to a self-contained, rustic, and very pretty casita. What had been an adventure for me had been absolute misery for Adrian, albeit done with a good heart. We were both glad to see it finished but for vastly different reasons.

How much does Grandad love you, Christian? He loves you *this* much!

Testicle Trees

Adrian and I aren't the world's best gardeners. It's not for the want of trying; we're just not any good at it. Every year I spend money on plants and shrubs and every year, despite good advice from my green-fingered in-laws, they fail. Weeds obstinately set themselves and flourish but I get a two-fingered salute from anything cultivated. They either die, get eaten by rabbits, or recognise the danger and decide not to stay. Perennials become annuals as they pack their bags at the end of the season and leave with not a trace of them to be seen from then on. One year I planted a mahonia and it thrived. I nursed it tenderly, proud of its healthy growth, and year after year I watched for its sweetly scented yellow flowers to appear. It grew to ten feet and then surprised us with a bumper crop of chestnuts. I'm just not cut out for this gardening lark.

Having a gardener hasn't entirely prevented a number of mishaps. When we arrived there was a huge, old, and gnarly apricot tree that had stood there for many years. It took one look at the new arrivals and gave up the ghost; tears of resin now run down its bark, branches are dying, and its sadness is palpable. It's clearly realised there's not much point in trying to carry on. The nectarine followed suit. Rafa tells us it's developed leprosy and is terminal. Its life spared for the moment, it now stands, warty and forlorn, in its quiet spot on the corner. And we've killed two of Rafa's four-bucket trees. We are, without a doubt, a disaster in any garden.

That isn't going to stop us trying.

The herb bed plumped up and seasoned a proliferation of wild rabbits. Sun-loving shrubs couldn't cope with the frying pan temperatures of Seville in summer and a gorgeous, orange-flowered climber, a gift from a friend, full-bloomed and fragrant, yellowed and died. It was labelled 'vigorous growth' so we were optimistic the ugly chain-link fence that separated the gardens would soon be ablaze with colour. We followed the care instructions religiously and watered it often. Unfortunately so did next door's dog.

We were determined we would plant something in our Spanish garden that would survive and, after scouring the internet for something that was hardy, can survive drought, isn't fussy about soil, likes full sun, and is Roberts-proof, we came up with an avocado tree.

Avocados are easy to grow apparently but don't fruit for five to seven years. That's a long time and I may not ever get to enjoy one. As Maggie Smith said in *The Best Exotic Marigold Hotel*, 'At my age, I don't plan that far ahead. I don't even buy green bananas,' so popping a stone over water and waiting for it to sprout, exciting as it sounds, is a non-starter for me. A trip to the garden centre was called for.

The garden centre on the road to Morón de la Frontera, one of our closest towns, is huge and lush with a vast array of plants, shrubs, and trees. Exotic plants that, at home in the UK, could only be houseplants were in glorious colourful bloom outside in the sun and some of them were enormous.

After losing myself for too long among the flowers, it was time to go look for the tree.

Avocados like a sub-tropical climate so I wasn't sure if I was pushing my luck so far inland. I found an assistant — a short, middle-aged man with the twinkle in his eye I've seen so often in Spain and which makes me wonder if Spanish men are born with a special gene for mischief. I should have been prepared.

'I'm looking for an avocado tree.'

'Ah.' Twinkle. '*Cojones.*'

What did he say?! Testicles? What did I say? What did I do? I looked around. There was no one else there; it must be me. Perhaps he was upset about something. He didn't look it. Quite the contrary; he seemed very happy with himself. I tried again.

'I'm sorry, excuse me. Can you help? I'm looking for an avocado tree.'

'*Sí, señora.*' Chuckle, big grin. '*Cojones.*'

Perhaps he had Tourette's. The Spanish for avocado is *aguacate*, nothing like *cojones*, and I knew my pronunciation really wasn't that bad. Perhaps he was pulling my leg.

'*Venga,*' he said, noticing my confused expression. 'Come with me.'

He crooked his finger and I followed. We walked a short distance away to an area with a lot of young trees, all different varieties and, in among them, just a few young avocados. *Ah, that's it, he hadn't misheard me. Must be Tourette's.*

'*Señora, aguacate,* avocado. These trees are two years old. Very good.'

In my mind was the fact that avocados don't fruit for five to seven years. If I bought one at two years old, I may still have to wait another five before they produced, assuming they, or I, survived that long. I wasn't going to take that chance.

'D'you have an older tree?'

'Older? You want an adult?'

'A bit more mature, yes, please.'

'Ah, the *señora* likes big *cojones*.' Chuckling again and leaning towards me with a wink, as he turned his back, his shoulders were shaking.

This is either his last day or he's on something. They sell cannabis compost here; I wonder just what else they may have hidden away. What sort of place have I come to?

'¡*Mire! Señora*, look!' He held out the ticket on the tree.

If there's fun to be had in any situation, you can guarantee the Spanish will find it and this time the fun was at my expense. I looked as instructed and there, on the label, green like the incredible hulk, was the biggest pair of *cojones* I've ever seen.

'*Señora*, you need two. He needs a girlfriend.'

And so it was that I ended up with two testicle trees and two very pink cheeks. At least I made someone's day.

A couple of days later, Rafa and Dolores arrived.

'Jean,' Rafa's round frame shaking with laughter, 'in *España* this tree is called...'

'Yes, Rafa. I know.'

Enjoying the Food

It wouldn't seem right to write a book about our time in Spain without mentioning both food and flamenco; they're such an integral part of the Spanish way of life.

Since the episode with the cook-in-sauce bag, we've sampled and cooked a huge variety of Mediterranean food. I'm an avid cook and Suzanne and I often cook together. I'm at my happiest when I'm looking after my family. I spent years working and missing out on family life so now I relish it and make the most of every minute. Michael says we're a family of 'feeders'. He's right, of course. Both my girls are excellent cooks and we do all tend to equate food with love. We love to spoil our family. For me, there's nothing better than a house full of family and friends and a table groaning with colourful, exciting, exotic dishes that have been lovingly prepared.

Having only previously holidayed at the coast where the food was, let's say, nice enough but geared towards pleasing tourists, I was surprised at the quality and variety of food inland. There were some surprises and some horrors but, overall, I've been equally surprised at how elegant and tastefully presented so much of it is, even in some of the smallest tapas bars. When we met up with friends in the tiny town of Almonte, we went to eat in a minuscule tapas bar in a little backstreet. The food served there wouldn't have been out of place in a high-end London restaurant but it was their standard fare and cost only two euros a plate. The quality and service were amazing.

Spicy food isn't well liked in Spain but what there is bursts with flavour and is full of colour. A long table in the outdoors, dotted with bowls of salad and jugs of wine and covered with plates of delicious tapas, is heavenly and such a feast for the eyes. Asking for salad in a restaurant unfortunately means you're more than likely to be served *ensaladilla*, a thick concoction of mayonnaise and diced vegetables. This was one of the shocks in the early days. Expecting a nice green, crispy salad, I was surprised when a small plate of gloop was placed in front of me. It tastes better than it looks but it definitely wasn't the salad I thought I'd ordered. Nowadays *ensalada verde* — green salad — is frequently found on a menu but in days gone by it was rarely heard of.

Food is a huge part of Spanish culture and Spanish people eat unashamedly all day long. Any get-together is an occasion for eating. Whole families go out to eat together and it's not unusual to see grandparents, aunties, uncles, parents, and children all crowding around a table at night for dinner. No one gets left behind and nobody gets left out of the conversation; children are seen *and* heard; everyone from the oldest to the youngest is included. Spanish society is nothing if not family-centric.

Tapas culture is strong in Andalusia. A stop for anything other than coffee invariably means being served a small dish of something, even if it's only olives or crisps. One evening we'd been into Acerico with Christian and Georgia, now his fiancée. We'd had a few cocktails in one bar and moved on to get something to eat. The only restaurant nearby was very quiet so I asked if the kitchen was open and was told no. By this time Georgia had scuttled off to the loo so we thought if we were using the facilities we ought to order something.

'Two cokes and two beers please.'

'¡*Vale*!' OK!

We sat. The drinks appeared and, with them, a huge bowl of crisps. The waiter had obviously taken pity on our hungry state. As we sipped our drinks, plate after plate of tapas arrived — calamari, prawns in garlic, wild boar, *ensaladilla*; they just kept on coming. Unasked for and unexpected and all so fresh. We could see the bartender cooking everything at the side of the bar. At the end we asked for the bill. It arrived with two bottles of liqueur, four glasses, and a charge for just the cokes and beer.

Adrian tallied up what it would have cost to provide all of these tapas and added it to the bill. There was no way we could take all of that for nothing. The bartender's response was to come back with a small gift for each of us; leather wallets for the men and a gadget that clips onto tables to hang a handbag for me and Georgia. Bad luck to put your handbag on the floor apparently; all your money will run out. Culture lesson also free of charge.

The national dish, or at least the dish most people associate with Spain, is paella. Paella isn't on the menu as much as would be expected and, if I'm honest, I've never really enjoyed it much in a restaurant so rarely, if ever, order it. Such a lot of it is mass-produced in factories in Valencia and sent out. We've found that, if it arrives in less than 30 minutes, it's definitely a freezer meal and has been reheated. It's best avoided.

For Spanish people, paella is generally a dish cooked for large family get-togethers and the correct way to eat it is straight from the dish it's cooked in. The *paellero* is placed on the table and everyone tucks in, starting from the outside and working towards the middle. The crust on the bottom is an additional delicacy; if it's not there, then the paella hasn't been cooked properly and you've been cheated. Traditionally, paella should only ever be eaten as a lunchtime meal and never at night.

For us, the best paella is cooked outside, in the open, over a fire. Nowadays it's gas burners rather than wood but the end result is the same. There's something about food cooked outdoors that always makes it taste better. In our family, and only in Spain, Adrian is the paella master. Laidback on a bar stool, beer in hand, he holds court around the *paellero*, stirring and mixing a perfect paella. It's a very social occasion and everyone gets a crusty bottom!

It was fiesta time again and we decided to go to the next village where a gigantic paella was going to be cooked. This amazing event happens all over Spain. The whole village gets together and cooks for several hundred people. When we arrived, there was already a crowd and the party had begun. Tables were groaning with bottles and picnics, families were gathering, friends were laughing together, and the whole feeling was carnival.

Buckets of peppers, garlic, and onions, were thrown into an enormous paella dish. It was eight to ten feet in diameter and the cooks constantly walked around the pan with a six-foot paddle held in both hands, continually moving and turning the mixture so that it didn't burn.

The vegetables sautéed in about a gallon of olive oil until it was time to add the tomatoes and the meat. Water and saffron next, and finally it was time to add the rice; all the while the cooks stirred constantly.

Meanwhile villagers were still turning up, groups of people meeting with friends and neighbours to form larger groups to laugh, chat, sing, dance, and party. Children ran around, being fussed and patted, fed candyfloss and popcorn, faces occasionally being wiped and stroked by immaculately dressed mothers. A clutch of giggling young girls sashayed past in their beautifully colourful flamenco dresses. The atmosphere was intoxicating.

Occasionally the cooks put down their beer for another stir. Those more dedicated to their art attempted to stir with one hand. Not a drop of beer was spilt. All the time, people crowded closely around the open fire, jostling to see what was going on.

The result was amazing; the best-ever paella, cooked and eaten al fresco and, best of all, it was free. A gift to the people. With the Spanish penchant for enjoying life, the entire event was a lot of fun. It was a big occasion, another excuse to party. Bring your own wine and you're good to go; a Spanish bring-a-bottle party.

There are many stories about how paella came about. Whether the Moors introduced it or it was invented by the Spanish as a cheap and convenient meal for workers in the rice fields is unclear but the tale I like best is the one about the poor cook who fell in love with the daughter of a Spanish noble. She had rich suitors but the poor cook had nothing to offer her. In his quest to make her a gift of something special, he took food from the earth and fish from the ocean and produced this exquisite dish which won her heart. He gave her the land and the sea. *Para ella*, for her. Paella. OK, paella is technically the pan it's cooked in but isn't it nice to imagine there was some romance in its origins?

I love to visit the local markets which are vibrant and fun, stuffed with delicious meat, cheese, fruit, vegetables, and fish, visually very exciting, and bustling with life. If you want to see how the Spanish live and eat, the market is the place to be. Often they've been there for decades and are housed in some amazing architecture with lots of arches and wrought iron. Stalls are hidden in alcoves and every turn brings another feast for the eyes and an assault on the senses. I've never been to a market in Spain that hasn't been an absolute delight.

Our local market isn't very big. It's old but, with its low ceilings, it's fairly dark inside and looks a bit run-down and claustrophobic. That doesn't change the quality and variety of food there. It has four entrances on two different streets and, regardless of where you enter, as you walk inside, you're met with an assortment of wonderful aromas. From the front, it's fish; from another entry, it's coffee; from another, the lovely garlicky smell of food cooking in the little cafés and bars dotted around the market. The bars are busy, with husbands sitting drinking small beers while their women shop, tapas are served, and the bustle and noise carry on.

The freshest of fruit and vegetables are sold in our local market. I've seen produce in these markets that I've never seen before and haven't a clue what to do with but there's never a shortage of people with helpful advice, a knowledgeable assistant or friendly housewife on hand to share her favourite way of cooking. Stalls piled high with fish so fresh they're almost wriggling and huge langoustines and prawns. Heads are left on fish so that you can see the eyes. If they don't sparkle, the women don't buy. Rows and rows of ham legs hang above counters, with tiny upside-down coolie hats underneath to catch any drips, the vendor advising on the best quality and how it should be cut and eaten. Wafer-thin slices with wine. Always with wine. Red wine.

Our market is so small it spills over onto the street with people who don't have a stall but are prepared to stand outside selling produce. There's the man who sells freshly cut herbs and produce from his allotment, and the lady who peels and sells prickly pears. Occasionally there's someone selling clothes, just as many as he can hang over his arm or that fill the small carrier bag at his feet.

The quality of food in supermarkets is excellent too. In our local Mercadona, the fish counter is vast. Mussels and gastropods are sold in net bags; whole, huge fish are displayed, still with their mouths open, gasping for air. It's the busiest part of the shop. The housewives crowd around the counter, jostling for position, prodding and poking, inspecting every piece, making sure they get the choicest part. They're not going to be fobbed off with rubbish; only the best will do.

The rest of the supermarket is fascinating — the biggest tins of tuna I've ever seen, pickled aubergines, spring onions bigger than a boiled egg, olive oil in gallon containers, and wine at less than a euro a bottle. It's a real Aladdin's cave.

Mercadona is also a coeliac's dream, a gluten-free heaven. All 'safe' products are clearly labelled and there's the biggest-ever range of gluten-free food, not just part of an aisle but across the entire shop. They even sell gluten-free baguettes that actually taste like bread.

I love to wander around supermarkets and there's not much missing from what I would buy at home. I prefer to cook Mediterranean when I'm in Spain anyway so I always try to go for local produce. The Mediterranean diet is known to be one of the healthiest in the world and the bonus is that Spanish life expectancy is one of the highest in Europe. Any diet that advocates drinking wine for good health sounds good to me.

One weekend we had friends coming to stay so I decided

on a mass tapas-cooking session, starting the day before. I'd stocked up with lots of fresh vegetables, fruit, and fish and started cooking up a storm. One of the dishes was a delicious roasted pepper and olive dish where a tablespoon of fino sherry was thrown in towards the end. It tasted wonderful. As the fridge was full by then, I covered it with foil and left it overnight. In the morning all the non-stick had peeled off the pan. So much for healthy eating.

Pass me another margarita instead. It's got a lime in it!

One Sunday morning our neighbour, Romero, called in to invite us to a pig killing at his brother's farm. I'd seen his brother and anything less like a farmer I couldn't imagine. Each time I've seen him, he's covered in paint and cement dust and, more often than not, propping up the bar.

'Where's his farm, Romero?'

'Not far, we can walk there.'

And then he added, 'On the road to Lora, about seven miles, not far.'

Just a gentle stroll then.

'Ah, Romero, it sounds wonderful but we're going home tomorrow.'

'¡Ay. No, que rabia!' What a pain. 'I tell my brother, "You bring the pig; I bring the Ingleses."'

Sounds like a good deal. 'Sorry, Romero.'

'No pasa nada. Pues, la próxima vez.' Don't worry, next time then. 'I save some morcilla.' A Spanish version of black pudding.

With a fair wind and a bit of good fortune, he might forget that offer.

Do I want to talk about the pig killing? Probably not but it's a big part of country life in Spain so I suppose I should.

Traditionally a knife goes into the pig and, if done properly, it's over quickly. However, this method has long been outlawed and, legally, the animal must be stunned first but this is the countryside and, unofficially, the tradition continues. In many parts of Spain, it seems the law is an optional extra.

The end of the year is the time for a pig killing, just in time to stock up for the Christmas festivities. Despite the invite we've never yet been to one. Now that we know when they do it, we'll make a point of not being around. I suppose we should man up and be more aware of where our food comes from before we see the sanitised version wrapped in cling film in the supermarkets but I'm happy in my ignorant bubble, thank you.

It's not that long ago since we were doing the same in the UK but my generation, and possibly the one before, have gone soft. Spanish country folk keep animals for the table and take responsibility for slaughtering and butchering them themselves. There's no sentimentality about killing food. They deal with it the way they deal with everything else, by having a party.

When it's time to kill the pig, friends and neighbours gather round to process the massive amount of meat. The meat is cured, sausages and chorizo are made, blood is drained to make *morcilla*, and the family larder is filled for the year.

No part of the pig is wasted — lard is used for cooking, hooves are boiled to make gelatine, and bones are ground for fertilizer. The only part of a pig that isn't used is its oink.

If it's done correctly, the animal has only a few feet to walk from where it's lived all its life and it's all over in seconds. No one wants to see the animal stressed out because the adrenalin affects the taste of the meat so it's kept calm until the last possible moment. There's no stress from being loaded onto lorries and driven to an abattoir.

All of this takes place over two days around St Martin's Day on the 11th of November. Two days of copious amounts of food, alcohol, and partying. It's part of Spanish country life and tradition. I respect it but I think I'll be avoiding Romero in November from now on.

Flamboyant Flamenco

We were invited by Austin to go to the carnival in Écija where there was going to be a big flamenco festival. I was excited because I'd only seen street performance flamenco, the type put on for tourists, or the occasional spontaneous and more authentic outbreaks in bars when someone would come in with a guitar and start playing, usually gentle at first and then someone would start clapping which invariably led to stamping, singing, and dancing. Very quickly the whole bar would be involved. The dancing would be rough, unpolished, gypsy style, performed with passion, wildly erotic, and accompanied by a voice that sounded like a primitive cry of agony coming from deep within the innermost soul of the singer. Chillingly exciting!

We drove to Écija early, having previously been caught out at carnival time when we'd stopped to allow a police car past only for him to pull in front of us and promptly close the road. This time we were prepared. We arrived early and found a good space in the empty car park. It was just a short walk to Austin's from there.

At eight we wandered over to the carnival ground. The

first things that struck us were the noise of the fairground and the smell of *churros*, the little pieces of fried choux pastry similar to, but lighter than, a doughnut. The carnival ground was festooned with bright, colourful, light displays and all around, in the midst of food and beer tents, were huge marquees for the dancing. There were men on horseback wearing the tightest of tight pants and short-fitted jackets topped off with a big black sombrero, and girls from toddlers to pensioners in bright, colourful flamenco dresses. They wore flowers in their hair and a great big smile. Those smiles were infectious and, by the end of the evening, my face was aching from smiling so much.

Inside the marquee the dancing and singing had already begun. Troupes of dancers were taking to the stage, each with its own dress and colours, and each with its own style of dance with stamping and stomping and fiery passion in each one. Elegant dancers with earnest young faces took to the stage and performed in faultless synchronisation, twirling, lunging, and clapping. Bongo-type drums played and then the cajón drummers, sitting on what looked like an oblong box, joined in to bang out a rhythm on it.

Throughout the marquee small groups of people and individuals in the audience joined in, dancing, swaying, stamping, lost in the music. A group of older ladies took to the stage wearing shawls crossed over their body and tucked into their waistbands. Skirts were twirled and shaken with incredible energy but the shawls remained. In the heat of that September evening, they didn't even break a sweat.

At midnight a troupe of young girls took to the stage. They could only have been eight to ten years old but the performance, and particularly at that time of night, was nothing short of stunning.

Not a castanet was seen all evening. Castanets are for Sevillanos and tourists. This was flamenco in the raw;

colourful, exciting, passionate. This was the real deal; it went behind the castanets and into the heart and soul of Spain.

The solo singers followed and we stayed to listen to a few. They were impassioned and heartfelt, some speaking of deep-seated struggle and agony. The crowd fell silent and, at the end of each song, rose to their feet and clapped vigorously and roared out a cheer. We felt like interlopers intruding on private sorrow and grief but, as there was only so much pain that our eardrums could take, we called it a day and left. It had been a magical evening.

Before heading home, we stopped for *churros*. Huge portions were served in plain white paper with a cup of thick chocolate for dipping. It reminded me of when I was young and eating fish and chips out of newspaper. Not having a sweet tooth, I passed on the chocolate but the *churros* were delicious, so light and fluffy.

On our way back to Austin's, we all stopped for supper in the early hours of the morning. The restaurant was full and an older man wearing a poncho and sombrero was playing the guitar and serenading the tables. Our friend Nick told him Adrian was a famous rock star from England. It took twenty minutes and several euros before he stopped begging Adrian for a song.

Hunting Season

From March onwards Adrian goes into killing mode. It's hunting season and no wasp is safe. He hunts queen wasps without mercy in an attempt to prevent any colony building and instantly destroys any that try to escape his eagle eye. From March until the end of August, he's rarely seen without an orange spray can attached to his right hand.

During our first summer in Acerico, Adrian destroyed more than 30 nests. No sooner was one demolished than construction started on another. There were hundreds and hundreds of wasps. In the dryness of summer, they would settle on anything floating in the pool to be able to get close to moisture, and a meal outside involved more time swatting than eating. We tried incense, citronella, and smoke bombs without any effect. While we choked on smoke and fumes, wasps happily buzzed in and out through the smoulder, thumbing their noses at us and settling on food and bodies. It was pretty unbearable at times. The only upside to this was that we got a lot of exercise running from the wasps; the only exercise anyone was getting in that heat.

The following year we started early and went for the

queens. We zapped them before they had a chance to build and those that escaped got knocked down as soon as the first sign of a nest appeared. It worked. When the queens arrive, they're already fertile and, over the course of a summer, can produce thousands of offspring. That was where the problem needed to be tackled so we geared up and went to war. The battle for Acerico commenced with the campaign to head off the enemy at the pass. In our war room planning, we decided that, as destroying the nests prevents new queens from being born, that's where the troops, i.e. Adrian, would be deployed.

We set traps around the garden with little effect so it seemed the only way to get rid of them would be to eliminate any place where they may get a foothold to build, not very easy in such a huge garden with an army of only two. We were outnumbered but we weren't going to be outmanoeuvred. We bought expanding foam and filled in holes, cut back hedges, and moved anything unnecessary from the pool to prevent wasps landing but there was still an incredible number of them.

We needed reinforcements so we brought in our grandson. Findley became the Waspfinder General with Adrian the Chief Exterminator, their mission to seek and destroy; Grandson and Granddad a formidable team. Chrystal took to sitting under mosquito netting beneath the pergola, pretending to be an Arabian princess. Despite, or maybe because of, her regal bearing, these evil little buggers were still smacking at the net trying to get in, mistaking her perhaps for another queen.

As we destroyed the nests and demolished new builds, one by one these horrid little Hymenopterans gave up the fight and disappeared, moving on to ruin someone else's summer. The battle to reclaim Acerico had been won and, for the last few years, we've seen very few wasps. Those that do appear are taking their lives into their own hands and we deal with them rapidly. The battle may have been won but the army hasn't been disbanded.

If we give up, they'll gain a foothold and become a problem again so we continue our quest for annihilation. Wasps are sneaky little devils so we stay on top of the game; any let-up and they would be back with a vengeance. They send out scouts and then arrive in droves. They have a mob mentality and, when they arrive, they come fully equipped, carrying small but powerful weapons, little kamikazes prepared for attack, ready to dive-bomb and sting without mercy. Their sting packs one heck of a punch and some are so venomous they've been known to kill.

Swatting a wasp doesn't help as it only attracts more of the blighters. A wasp in danger gives off pheromones and sends out a signal to the rest of its colony and they come in swarms so killing one wasp just attracts all its mates who come booted and tooled up ready for battle. They aren't beautiful; they aren't useful and they don't have the same fascination as bees. They're sadistic little beasts whose only purpose is destroying and terrorising our summer. In my opinion the only good wasp is a dead wasp. Dead and incinerated.

I fail to see the point of wasps and haven't yet found a useful purpose for their existence. They're meant to kill other bugs and flies but there are zappers for that if you want and, to be honest, bugs and flies are much less of a nuisance than these angry little thugs.

One of the bugs they kill are bees. Friendly, lovely, cuddly, non-threatening bees. Bumblebees float around just looking gorgeous in their fur coats, a fluffy ball of loveliness, completely harmless, completely enchanting, dopey and ditzy flying beauties, the blondes of the bee family. Wasps feed on bugs; bees feed on pollen. Without bees to pollinate, the planet would not survive. We need our honey bees.

Wasps destroy our lovely bees and also invade hives to eat the honey. In our area, beekeepers keep beehives in the olive groves and fending off the wasps is a constant battle. They're attracted to the sweetness of the honey and the bees will fight to the death to defend their home. Wasps are aggressive little fighters and can quickly wipe out an entire colony of bees. They're the spawn of the devil!

During our first summer in Acerico, we watched in horror as a couple of wasps caught a beautiful dragonfly mid-air, brought it down, and started to eat it alive. Oh yes, I can justify eliminating wasps and eliminating places where they can build a nest. They deserve to die. I will happily buy Adrian as many orange spray cans as he wants and stand by his side as he takes aim. Sod the environment!

We now seem to be on top of the problem. By not allowing them to nest, they go somewhere else. Last year we only found the beginnings of two nests. We obliterated them and we were finally wasp-free. We had no more guests squealing, flapping, screaming, and jumping into the pool to escape. Now we can bathe in blissful peace.

There's a proper name for fear of wasps — Spheksophobia, also known as self-preservation. You understand by now I'm not a lover of wasps. I would rather take on a rabid dog. Just my opinion of course but, while there's a chance of a single wasp invading our space, the army hasn't been stood down and remains on alert for immediate mobilisation whenever necessary.

Chrystal? Even though we're now relatively wasp-free, she still loves to be treated like a princess.

The Bullfight Dilemma

Spending an afternoon watching a man in a fancy suit facing down half a ton of angry pot roast isn't my idea of entertainment. A bullfight is never going to find its way onto my bucket list.

Around Morón are several farms that breed fighting bulls. These animals are pampered and get the very best of care right to the point of taking them to the bullring. They're bred for aggression and strength and live in lush surroundings before they see the ring at about four years old. Because of their ultimate destination, they're valuable and thus live a much better life than animals in the UK and, it can be cautiously argued, have a better death. They at least go down fighting. That doesn't mean I agree with it. I most certainly don't but it's an argument nonetheless.

There's still a bullring in Morón and there's a festival every year, however the graffiti on the wall shows everyone doesn't welcome it. It reads *'Tortura. Ni arte. Ni cultura.'* Torture. Neither art. Nor culture.

No way of slaughtering animals is pretty. I'm not a vegetarian. I wear leather shoes and carry leather handbags and the country I come from supports chasing terrified foxes and frightened rabbits to the point of exhaustion and then tearing them apart while they're still alive so, as much as I dislike bullfighting and however gory and horrific I find it, I'm not going to be hypocritical and criticize another country's centuries-old tradition.

Some years ago I would have been a fierce opponent of bullfighting and would have seen it as a barbaric and inhumane practice. That was in the days before most of our meat in the UK became halal compliant, basically meaning the poor creature has its throat cut and is left to bleed to death. Some slaughterhouses claim the animal is stunned first but, to comply with the laws governing halal, stunning isn't allowed. This causes unnecessary suffering and is unbelievably cruel.

Almost every major supermarket in the UK sells meat that's killed by halal methods and the majority of consumers are unaware of this fact. To pacify a small minority of the population, animals are put through unspeakable and unimaginable agony and terror. As a nation of animal lovers, we sit back and say nothing about this but are outraged by bullfighting.

Somehow, in comparison, the bullfight doesn't seem so bad. Apart from the cruelty, my main objection is that it's done for enjoyment, for entertainment. Watching an animal die shouldn't be fun, especially when it dies in pain. The Spanish would argue that the bull doesn't suffer and, indeed, they're genuinely unhappy when it isn't a clean kill. The coup de grâce should be a clean blow with a sword through the shoulder blades into the heart and the bull should die immediately. If it doesn't, the crowd are in uproar; there's a genuine dissatisfaction that this valiant beast hasn't met a fitting end.

Adrian grew up on a farm and he says the cows knew

when they were going to slaughter and were terrified. It was a distressing sight. Bulls are dangerous animals and these fighting bulls are bred for aggression. They certainly don't show the same fear as those being shunted off to the abattoir on the back of a lorry. Those animals know they're going to die. In the ring the bull has a fighting chance, even if it's very one-sided. When a bull charges out into the ring, the last thing on his mind is that he's going to die. He wants to kill the matador who stupidly thinks it's a skill to taunt a dangerous beast. Occasionally he succeeds.

When a bull is killed, the crowds cheer; when a matador is gored, the crowds cheer and sometimes shout for the bull's life to be spared. The bull is seen as brave, is returned to his life of being pampered and lives out his days in happy retirement siring other brave bulls for the ring. The con is that this is a reward for the bravery of the animal. The truth is that the bull wouldn't be allowed to fight again because it's learnt from its time in the ring and is now far too dangerous.

There's a huge groundswell of opinion in Spain arguing against bullfighting. However in Andalusia it's still going strong. The majority of bullrings are still in use but, optimistically, some have closed. It's been outlawed completely in some places. Bullrings are being allowed to fall into disrepair, are being demolished or repurposed. Some have been made into offices, some into museums, some into art galleries.

Thousands of people in Spain have recently taken to the streets to protest against the cruelty of killing bulls in this way and Catalonia has banned it altogether. The Balearic Islands have introduced a law that bans the harming or killing of bulls during bullfights and have instituted some major changes stating that only three bulls instead of six are to be used in any fight and are only allowed in the ring for ten minutes at a time. Less of a bullfight, more of a bull tease. It's a step in the right direction yet the government in Madrid are trying to overturn the ban as it's 'unconstitutional'.

I would like to think the bullfight is a dying pastime but I'm afraid it's not. In Andalusia, old habits die hard. It's not unusual for fights to be televised and the programme even shown on the local buses. It's still very popular and it still pulls in the crowds.

There was no bullring in El Nacarino but I remember the frisson of excitement when the travelling bullring came to town. It arrived with all the hoopla that a travelling circus attracts and people were buzzing. There were an equal number who didn't want to know.

Me? I said nothing. I'm living in a glass house and I'm not throwing any stones but, when two bullfighters were gored and killed, it was hard to summon up any sympathy. On his way to hospital, one of them, Iván Fandiño, complained of being in pain. Really? A taste of what the bull suffers perhaps. I'm not joyful at their deaths but I can't claim to be sorry either. They did kind of ask for it.

While most of us find the bullfight barbaric and abhorrent, some people in Spain are equally dismissive of us because of their perceived attitude of us Brits towards our children. At the end of our road in El Nacarino, there lived a small, excitable, but very friendly brown and white dog with its small, excitable, very friendly owner. I was on my way one day to the *Guardia Civil*, down the steps just past the house, when the dog bounded out of the open door and bounced all over me.

'¡*Ay, Inglesa*! You like my dog.' Lola had followed her dog out of the house and wanted to chat.

Despite almost bowling me over each time I walked past, yes, I did like her dog. '*Sí*, I like him very much.'

'Why you no like children?'

'I do like children, Lola. What makes you say that?'

'No, *los Ingleses* don't like children. My sister tell me. They like dogs.'

Oh dear. I can see where this is going and it isn't going to go well; I don't really want to be getting into this.

With a determined set to her jaw, Lola continued, 'My sister has friend who went to London. She say *los Ingleses* are *mala gente*, bad people. They beat children and they leave them.'

'Well, no...'

'She say *los Ingleses* give their children away and buy *animales*.'

'No, no. That's not right.'

'*Sí, Sí, es verdad,*' Yes, it's true. 'My sister tell me.'

She carried on in this vein for a while. She was very dismissive of working mums who leave their children because 'they can't be bothered with them', of parents who don't take their children anywhere. 'In London there are no children. Their parents hide them.'

'Lola, that's not right. English people love their children very much and care for them the same as in Spain; there's no difference.'

There was no point in continuing this conversation. She was convinced so, with a '*venga, hasta luego*', goodbye and see you later, and a peck on each cheek, I left Lola to contemplate the differences in international parenting and continued my walk. As I got to the top of the steps, Lola called after me, 'Come and play with my dog any time you want.'

It was a friendly encounter but it left me feeling shocked at how we're perceived. In twenty years as a childcare social worker, I saw all sorts of depravity and cruelty and it was across the board. Social class and nationality didn't come into it. We're genuinely not worse than any other nation and we're a darned sight better than some. Mostly it's just a difference in perception.

While the Spanish child is pampered, revered, and indulged, our local brothel here in Spain was closed for eighteen months for using under-aged trafficked girls. In effect, children. I was horrified that the same men who were so indulgent and loving towards their own children could be happy to have sex with underage foreign girls.

I have no plans to ever go to a bullfight but then I don't plan ever to visit an abattoir either. There was a scene in the 1970s sit-com *Duty Free* where the character Amy Pearce refers to a matador as a hitman for Fray Bentos. I couldn't put it better myself.

Sex Sells

Sex is big business in Spain. Every town has its brothel and they proliferate along the motorways. Some are very discreet but most are very obvious and advertise themselves unashamedly. In this Catholic country, with bright neon lighting and enough red lights to stop aircraft, there appears to be no stigma attached to these clubs.

It's estimated that more than one in four Spanish men visit a prostitute at some time in their lifetime and it was recently reported that approximately 100,000 men in Majorca visit prostitutes every year. That's a big number for such a small island.

Will the need for prostitution diminish as life for the younger Spanish becomes free of some of the restraints of the past? Possibly, but there's still a lot of money to be made from women who've been trafficked into the sex trade here. While prostitution isn't legal, it isn't illegal either and therefore it's not regulated and it's estimated that the greatest proportion, up to 90%, of the women sex workers in Spain have been trafficked. That's a lot of money being made, quite literally, on the backs of others. As it's neither legal nor illegal, it's a profession in limbo, somewhere between the devil and the deep blue sea.

The old taboos, along with Franco, have by and large disappeared. Birth control is freely available. Condoms are sold openly in garages and supermarkets and, in some cases, as in our nearby town, from slot machines on the wall outside the local pharmacy and available 24 hours a day. Spain's fourth emergency service.

While young, unmarried couples are still separated inside the home, it's no holds barred when outside, to the extent that the mayor of one Spanish town suggested turning off the car park lights for an hour each evening so that youngsters could get it on. In a town close to us, the car park has been brightly illuminated at night so they can't. There was so much activity, it was becoming a problem.

I have no issue with prostitution as long as it's through choice but I'm a fierce opponent of sex by coercion. Some women do choose this profession but the majority are the victims of circumstance, many of them trafficked. Our local brothel has now re-opened but the neon signs have disappeared and, most often, not even the red light is switched on. It's been painted hot pink but, overall, it's much more discreet. The only indicator that it's still in business is the full car park at the nearby café. The car park is full but the café is empty. The girls who work in the club can often be seen eating in the café and, at carnival time, are at the fairground, handing out leaflets advertising the club but they're never alone. There's always a man from the club with them or standing close by.

In our local club, the only car seen coming or leaving is the owner's. The girls don't arrive for work, do a shift, clock off, and go home. It's quite unsettling to walk past in the sunshine, believing there are girls inside who don't have the freedom to walk outside the door.

A large percentage of sex workers in Spain are on the streets. For a variety of reasons, they either choose not to use, or are not acceptable in, the clubs. Despite it being socially accepted, it's not, and never will be, a safe way of earning a living for the girls on the street. Notwithstanding exploitation, the brothels offer a level of safety the street girls will never experience. Some of them offer a degree of luxury and comfort that's welcomed. The girls who are working legitimately and willingly in the clubs have the security of legal acceptance where prostitutes are granted workers' rights, benefits, and employment contracts. This doesn't apply to girls who have been trafficked.

Possibly because of this liberalised attitude towards sex, the rape statistics for Spain compared to the rest of the world are fairly low. It appears the general behaviour of violence towards women in Spain is changing. It was once said that the place where a Spanish woman was the least safe was in her own home. This was during a time when a strongly patriarchal culture ruled the country, where marriages were arranged and women were subservient. During the rule of Franco, women were repressed and men controlled every aspect of a woman's life from the moment she was born until the day she died. This was supported by a strong Catholic church who did nothing to lessen the burden women carried. With the death of Franco, this misery for Spanish women came to an end and, today, a young Spanish woman is more likely to be seen building a career than pushing a pram. Marriage and childbirth are through choice, not obligation. They are free and relishing that freedom.

Sex continues to be big business but it's more likely to be a foreign worker on the street or in the clubs than a Spanish woman and those working in the industry are no longer the outcasts they were in days gone by.

Where else but Spain would prostitutes be given up for

Lent? About 500 years ago, Felipe the Second visited Salamanca and was shocked at the low morals and debauchery of the students in the town so, with Lent about to start, he sent the prostitutes across the River Tormes where they stayed under the watchful eye of a priest for 40 days and 40 nights when a boat was sent to bring them back. On the day they returned, the Monday after Easter, they were met by the students who jubilantly held a big orgy on the riverbank — food, wine, song, and lots of sex, followed by a swim in the river.

Nowadays this event is still remembered and celebrated on the Monday after Easter, hence the name *Lunes de Agua*, Monday Water, but is rather tame in comparison. The whole town still closes down but, rather than a riverbank orgy, families and friends meet for picnics and parties. There's possibly not a lot of sex involved, not in the open air anyway.

Spain has also opened its first brothel in Barcelona where punters pay for having sex with anatomically correct dolls which come with the promise that they're always washed and disinfected after use.

On a lighter note, the luxury of these clubs occasionally throws up a funny side. Our local club has double doors leading to the smartest bar locally. These doors aren't often left open but occasionally, when they are, we've seen inside and it's very plush indeed. A friend tells me the place has often caused giggles and embarrassment to tourists who've wandered into the club and ordered a drink. One visitor, who walked in with his wife, was told in limited English that it was a club. When they asked if they could join and said they didn't mind paying, the owner pointed to the girls lining the walls. '*Señor, es un club.*' The penny dropped and, with burning faces, they hot-footed it back to the safety of their accommodation.

Elaine

'Hello, I'm your stalker.'

No, that's not what I said but I might as well have done. Since we'd moved out into the countryside, I'd missed seeing people, the general day-to-day interaction with other members of the human race. In El Nacarino, as soon as the door was open, there were neighbours; very friendly neighbours. One minute the street was empty and the next, as soon as we were spotted, people were popping out of every doorway. It could take quite some time to get to the end of the road and even longer if we had a grandchild with us. A walk into town had to have factored into it time allowed for chatting. It could be frustrating at times but, overall, it was one of the charms of living in a Spanish village. Here it's different. In our little group of houses, most people are weekenders who are friendly when we see them but aren't here very often. All are Spanish, apart from the Danes next door who still refuse to acknowledge our existence.

For a long time, I'd been saying we needed to meet people nearby. We had friends and a good social life but, because of where we are, they're all a drive away. There's no one close so we're pretty much isolated. Most of the time that suits us fine but it would be nice to have some outside contact occasionally. There's very little around our neighbourhood other than a few scattered houses, a motorway services, and the brothel. A Google map showed a B&B which was English owned and supposedly next to the brothel. I'd never seen a house in that location but I'd never really looked.

A quick check on Google showed it was run by 'the marvellous Elaine' and came with rave reviews for both the setting and the hostess.

'Just knock on her door and introduce yourself,' Adrian suggested. 'If she's as friendly as everyone says, she'll be pleased to see you.'

'You think so?'

'She's hardly likely to turn you away.'

After all the years we've been together, he can still amaze me at times.

'Hello, Adrian, let me introduce myself. I'm your wife of 30 years. Have we met yet? Oh, and by the way, in case you didn't know, I'm English. We don't *do* that sort of thing.'

I might walk past the house a couple of times on the off-chance and, you know, just see whom I might bump into, but knock on a stranger's door? No way, José. Adrian and I could just carry on in our happy, contented twosome for a while longer.

One morning during the renovation of the chicken coop, I was distracted from the internet and sent into the men's part of the Chinese *Todo* shop in Acerico to buy a plug socket. The *Todo* shops are very common in Spain and, as the name says, they sell *todo* — everything. A little like Poundland, still cheap but at varying prices. If you've ever been into one of these shops, you'll know exactly how stuffed and, sometimes, confusing they can be. There were about twenty different types of plug sockets.

I phoned Adrian to check on what to buy and, as I was talking, I noticed a woman hovering... listening... getting closer... and there it was, the approach.

'I've been looking for one of these for ages,' she said.

A multi-plug circuit breaker. What a basis for a friendship. A short exchange of small talk and then a light began to glimmer, followed by a thunderous great Sagittarian foot in mouth outburst of, 'Are you Elaine? I've been checking you out on the internet this morning.'

Ever had one of those moments when it's out before you can stop it? *OMG! I've never seen this woman before and I've just told her I'm stalking her. Please let me die right now. Please let the ground open up and swallow me. Please rewind the clock and pretend I didn't say that!*

Did she run? Did she look afraid? No, she didn't even threaten me with the *Guardia*. Instead she gave me her phone number.

Already got it. I've been stalking you, remember?

From that dodgy beginning has grown a lovely friendship. Elaine is everything the reviews say she is. She's warm-hearted, kind, generous, and funny, an excellent cook, and obviously a risk-taker.

Inviting Elaine to dinner or coffee automatically means making space for an extra dish — a few muffins, summer fruits with amaretto, always something deliciously homemade. It's not expected but 'it's what I do' she says. If Elaine had been at the last supper, she would have taken a casserole. Top quality, cordon bleu, of course.

Through Elaine we've learnt a lot about our local area and met so many interesting people. Life is never dull around her. A dinner party here, a shopping trip there, a chat over coffee. With anyone else these could be just mundane but the air around Elaine fizzes with excitement. Elaine makes things happen. She is bright, bubbly, and fun to be with. She is, as the reviews say, marvellous.

Elaine lives alone with her dog, Angel. Whatever pain, heartache, or loneliness she feels are kept to herself and there's no self-pity. She just gets on with life, always with a laugh bubbling away just below the surface, ready to burst out at any time.

It's amazing what you can pick up in these *Todo* shops.

It turned out that Elaine's home is a huddle of buildings at the end of a quiet lane off the A92, nowhere near the brothel. Flanked by a small farm on one side and a field of sweetcorn on the other, it's a peaceful and welcoming retreat. The only sounds you'll hear are the bleating of goats, birdsong, and Elaine's laughter. I promise you will get the warmest welcome anywhere in Andalusia.

In the last year, Elaine has made some major changes to her property. It's no longer a B&B but a smart and swanky self-catering, three-bedroom villa for rent. Absolutely superb, five-star luxury.

www.villalosparaisos.co.uk

Feeling Loved

I go and sit on the margarita bench in the orange grove. I nurse a glass of wine and listen to the silence. Laughter and the chink of glasses float across from the pool and I reflect on how lucky and how happy I am.

It wasn't always like this. In the dark days of social services, I frequently felt as if I were spiralling down into a deep pit that there was no way out of. Those days are long gone and nowadays those horrible memories seldom resurface. I no longer have nightmares, waking in the night sweating and frightened. Coming out of that didn't make me stronger. Instead it left me emotionally dependent and insecure but it pulled my family tighter around me and I found out who my real friends are. They're still with me. Between them they quite literally saved my life. Now I am at ease; I am content. The past cannot touch me.

It's not as important to have a lot of people around me as before. It's important to have the ones that matter and tonight they are right here — my two amazing daughters, their husbands whom I adore, my handsome grandsons, and the mermaid swimming in my pool, my lovely beautiful Eva.

Christian is engaged to be married. He's chosen well and, as the family grows, the love expands. We are good together. And Adrian, my strength, my rock, my love. Where would I be without you? It took a crisis for me to appreciate fully what I already had in life. I am more than lucky. I am blessed.

I love Spain and I hope that has come through. I love the spectacular scenery, the way the light seems brighter and clearer, making colours more vivid. I love that the smells are different, that the people are warm and welcoming. I love their liveliness, sociability, and overall happiness and I love the way I feel when I am here. Yes, love is the right word for all of this. I love Spain. I love it all.

And you know what? It feels as if it has loved me right back.

Recipes

Mantecados

Millions of Spanish people surely can't be wrong. These *mantecados* and *polvorones* are so loved throughout Spain that it's worth sharing the recipe, especially as their production has been the salvation and the lifeblood of my much-loved El Nacarino. I prefer them made with butter instead of lard but, if you want an authentic taste, then lard it has to be. They're simplicity itself to make.

Ingredients
8 oz (200 g) lard (or margarine/butter)
8 oz (200 g) caster sugar
2 egg yolks
Grated zest of 1 lemon
1 lb (400 g) of flour, sieved. (Recipe says plain but I've used self-raising and they've been perfectly OK.)
8 oz (200 g) ground almonds
1 tbsp (15 ml) ground cinnamon
Juice of 1 lemon (optional).

Method

Make sure the lard is soft and whisk it with the sugar, egg yolks, and lemon zest until soft and fluffy.

Beat in the flour, almonds, and cinnamon to make a soft dough. Add the lemon juice if using.

Roll out the dough to approximately ¾ inch thick and cut into small oval shapes. Place on a greased baking tray.

Bake at 400F/200C/gas mark 6 for 15-20 minutes and then turn down the oven to 350F/180C/gas mark 4 for another 15-20 minutes until golden.

Cool on a wire rack.

Makes 12 to 16.

Patatas a lo Pobre

My biggest addiction foodwise is for *patatas a lo pobre*, poor man's potatoes. It's the simplest and most basic of all Spanish dishes and, quite frankly, it's the nectar of the gods. I could eat it every day. The ingredients are simple and easily adjusted to cater for the number of people. It doesn't matter if the measurements aren't exact; this dish is foolproof.

Ingredients
1 large onion, sliced
1 green pepper, cut into strips. (I prefer green for this dish but red is perfectly OK.)
2 cloves of garlic, sliced
2 bay leaves
1 lb (400 g) of potatoes, peeled and sliced. (It doesn't work well with new potatoes.)
Salt and pepper
7 fl oz (200 ml) olive oil.

Method

Cover the bottom of a large pan with oil. When warm, add the onions and pepper. Cook until soft and add garlic, bay leaves, and potatoes. Season with salt and pepper.

Cover and simmer until the potatoes are cooked. Stir occasionally to prevent burning.

Drain off the oil, remove the bay leaves, and serve the potato mixture.

Feeds 4 as a main, served with salad, or more if served with pork or chicken or as tapas.

Save the wonderfully flavoured oil for use in another dish.

When I'm busy, I chuck the whole lot in a baking dish and put it in the oven at a low heat (320F/160C/gas mark 3), just checking in occasionally to make sure it doesn't roast and giving it a quick stir. Not the traditional way of doing it but oh so easy and just as yummy.

Doris's Lucky Escape – Kyra's Chicken Casserole

Ingredients
1 chicken, jointed and cut into chunks
14 oz (400 g) jar passata (tomato and garlic sauce)
7 oz (200 g) jar white haricot or cannellini beans, drained
36 fl oz (1 ltr) chicken stock
1 onion, chopped
3 cloves garlic, chopped
Seasoned flour
Olive oil
1 red pepper, sliced
1 yellow pepper, sliced
Handful of black olives, sliced (optional).

Method
Coat the chicken in the seasoned flour.
Cover the bottom of a large pan with olive oil and quickly fry the chicken on all sides to seal in the juices. Remove and put to one side.
Fry the onion, peppers, and garlic until soft and put into a casserole dish with the passata, chicken stock, and beans. If

using the olives, add them. Place the chicken on top of the mixture and cover.

Cook at 350F/180C/gas mark 4 for 40 minutes. Remove cover and return to oven for another hour to finish cooking and reduce some of the liquid.

Serves 4 generous portions.

Croquetas (Croquettes)

I used to make this dish when the children were young and money was tight. A little goes a very long way and my girls loved them. This is very much a 'make it up as you go along' recipe and almost any combination of ingredients can go in as long as the basic white binding sauce is used. More often than not, I used leftover chicken or ham and added sweetcorn or a handful of frozen peas and they made a filling and tasty meal. When I first came to Spain, I was surprised to find these pretty much as a staple, fed not only to children but also served in bars as tapas. Typical Spanish *croquetas* use Serrano ham as a filling so, if you want to stay traditional, use that, otherwise feel free to experiment.

Ingredients
2 oz (50 g) butter or margarine
2 oz (50 g) plain flour
½ pint (250 ml) milk
6 oz (150 g) cooked ham, chopped
2 oz (50 g) sweetcorn

4 oz (100 g) fresh white breadcrumbs
1 egg, beaten
Salt and pepper
Olive oil or an oil of your choice.

Method

First make the white sauce. Melt the butter in a saucepan and then add the flour. Cook gently for 1 minute, stirring all the time. Make sure the flour is mixed in well and the mixture doesn't have any lumps. It should make a nice, thick, glossy paste.

Remove the pan from the heat and gradually stir in the milk, stirring continually to keep it smooth. Return to the heat and bring to the boil slowly, stirring all the time. The mixture should start to thicken. Simmer gently for another 2-3 minutes until it's really thick and then season with salt and pepper.

Remove from heat and stir in the ham and sweetcorn.

Set aside to cool. It's best to transfer the mixture to a separate bowl as, if it's left in the hot pan, it will continue to cook.

When cool, take small portions of the mix and shape into croquettes, either small tube shapes or flatter rounds. Dip these in the beaten egg and then straight into the breadcrumbs to coat.

Fry in hot oil until golden on each side.

Makes 8. For tapas, make smaller croquettes. This amount is sufficient for 12 tapas portions.

Citrus Cordial

We're lucky enough to have an abundance of citrus fruit every year and so are easily able to make gallons of this. I make it because Adrian likes a cordial and we find it very difficult to buy in Spain.

Ingredients
2 lemons
1 orange
2 pints (1 ltr) water
12 oz (300 g) sugar
1 tsp (5 ml) citric acid.

Method
Peel the rinds from the lemons and orange, making sure not to leave any pith attached.
Peel the pith away from the fruit and discard.
Cut the fruit into quarters and put into a liquidiser with the rinds and ½ pint of water. Blitz for 10 seconds.
Put the liquidised mix into a saucepan and add the rest of the

water, sugar, and citric acid. Bring to the boil, stirring to dissolve the sugar. When dissolved, boil for 2 minutes. Remove from heat and leave to cool.

When cold, strain, bottle, and refrigerate.

Dilute to taste for drinking.

Freezes well for up to 3 months.

Austin's Spicy Cauli Burgers

Ingredients
1 medium cauliflower
6 oz (150 g) white breadcrumbs (approx.)
4 oz (100 g) gram (chickpea) flour plus 2 oz (50 g) for coating
2 eggs
1 tsp (5 ml) black pepper
1 tsp (5 ml) paprika
Pinch of salt
Small bunch fresh coriander, chopped, or 1 tsp (5 ml) dried.

Method
De-stalk the cauliflower and blend in food processor until it's the consistency of rough flour.
Put in a bowl. Whatever quantity it makes, add ⅓ of that amount of breadcrumbs, 4 oz (100 g) gram flour, pepper, paprika, and salt.
Mix together with as much liquid as you need from 2 eggs to bring it to the consistency of an uncooked burger.
Form into burger shapes. Mix the reserved gram flour with the coriander and coat the burgers.

Chill for at least an hour and then cook. These are suitable for shallow frying, BBQ, grilling — any way a normal burger would be cooked.

Makes 8.

Bill's Matrimonio Tapa

Matrimonio is Spanish for marriage and, although the ingredients may not seem an obvious match, I've been making this tapa ever since Bill served it when we went to visit him in El Nacarino. Whenever I do, I chuckle at the memory of being escorted out of town by his bearded friend on a shocking pink unicycle. Good times.

Ingredients for 1
1 slice thickly cut bread, toasted
Large tomato, sliced
A few strips of red pepper, roasted. (From a jar is OK.)
A few brown, salted anchovies
A few white, salted anchovies
1 tbsp olive pâté, preferably black (optional).

Method
Spread the toast with the olive pâté (if using).
Place a slice of tomato, a couple of strips of pepper on the

bread and criss-cross the brown and white anchovies on the top.

There it is, simplicity and happy memories combined.

This is a recipe for 1 *matrimonio*; keep multiplying it for however many you need.

My Own Bolognese Sauce

Well, it's Luisella's actually but, over the years, I've laid claim to it and I cook this recipe frequently when we're in Spain as it's both easy and delicious. Many years ago I had an Italian student, Luisella, staying with me and I had the nerve to try to cook her a spaghetti bolognese. When she saw what I was doing, she threw her hands up in horror and took over. So here it is, a bonafide, pure-bred Italian bolognese recipe courtesy of the lovely Luisella. It's the best!

Ingredients
18 oz (450 g) minced beef
1 large onion, chopped
2 cloves garlic, crushed
1 tbsp (15 ml) tomato purée
2 x 14 oz (2 x 400 g) cans chopped tomatoes
Salt and pepper
Olive oil for frying
12 oz (300 g) spaghetti (or more for hungry people!)

Method

Gently fry the onion and garlic in the olive oil until soft. Add the minced beef and fry until brown then pour away the fat. Stir in the tomato purée. Cook a few seconds longer then add the tinned tomatoes.

Season with salt and pepper and simmer for 15-20 minutes.

While the sauce is simmering, prepare the spaghetti according to the instructions on the packet.

Pour bolognese over cooked spaghetti.

This is a huge amount to feed a big Italian family and feeds 4 people, or more if you serve with larger portions of spaghetti. Eat some and freeze the rest or halve the quantities of mince and tomatoes. Lovely, tomatoey, northern Italian goodness which tastes delicious wherever you eat it.

¡*Buen apetito*!

Albondigas (Meatballs)

Another Spanish staple that also doubles up as a tapa.

Ingredients
Meatballs
½ lb (200 g) minced beef
1 medium onion, finely chopped
1 oz (25 g) fresh white breadcrumbs
1 egg, beaten
Salt and pepper
2 tbsps (30 ml) olive oil for frying.

Sauce
14 oz (400g) can chopped tomatoes
1 small onion, chopped
1 tsp (5ml) dried mixed herbs
1 tbsp (15ml) olive oil.

Method
Mix together the minced beef, onion, breadcrumbs, and egg

with plenty of salt and pepper. Squidge together until everything is well combined.

Divide the mixture into small pieces about the size of a walnut and roll each into a ball.

Heat the oil and fry the meatballs on all sides until browned. Place snugly into an ovenproof dish.

To make the sauce, heat the oil in a small saucepan and fry the chopped onion until just turning golden.

Add the tomatoes and herbs. Bring to the boil then reduce to a simmer for approximately 10 minutes or until the liquid has reduced.

Pour over the meatballs and place in a preheated oven at 350F/180C/gas mark 4 for 30 minutes.

For a spicy meatball dish, replace the mixed herbs with chilli powder.

Makes 12 to 16 meatballs.

Message from the Author

I sincerely thank you for reading this book and hope you enjoyed it. I would be extremely grateful if you could leave a review on Amazon. The sequel will be published next year so please follow me on Facebook or via my blog to be among the first to be notified of publication.

I'd also love to hear your comments and am happy to answer any questions you may have, so do please get in touch with me by:

- Email: jean@jeanroberts.me.uk
- Facebook: www.facebook.com/jean.roberts.775
- Website: www.jeanroberts.me.uk

If you enjoy reading memoirs, I recommend you pop over to Facebook group We Love Memoirs to chat with me and other authors. www.facebook.com/groups/welovememoirs

Acknowledgements

When I set out to write this, I had no idea where it would end up. It was just a set of diary entries and I guess I got carried away. Some of it surprised me in its unexpectedness. I didn't intend mentioning social services but there it is and, somehow, writing about it has laid a lot of ghosts. It's been strangely cathartic. I suppose I should thank them. Without my time there, the house in Spain wouldn't have happened and neither would this book. They unnecessarily and cruelly put me through the most painful and debilitating period of my life. There are no thanks for that.

My thanks do go, however, to my family and my dear friends who carried me at a time when I was barely able to function. They saved my sanity and my life. I am forever grateful.

Thank you to my daughter Suzanne Flynn for time spent reading, suggesting, and preventing me from offending too many people; to Kate Strong for suggestions on punctuation and chicken feeding; to Jenny Pennick who read, laughed, and encouraged; and to Austin, Dolores, Rafa, and Elaine who have all helped to make our time in Spain so much fun. There are many, many more not mentioned in the book who have enriched our lives in one way or another. Spain wouldn't be the same without you.

A big thank you goes to our talented granddaughter, Eva, for coming up trumps in an emergency and providing the caricature of a wasp, to my father-in-law, Brian, who provided some of the drawings, and to our photographer friend, Nick Moore, for allowing me to use the flamenco and Penitents photos on my website. We may have been at the same events but your photos are way better than mine.

Special thanks go to Sarah Banham who told me I could do it. Your support was invaluable at a very wobbly time. Thanks to Heather Purdey who introduced me to Sarah; to Jacky Donovan who had faith enough in me to commit to print; and to my husband, Adrian, who had badgered me for years to get on and write. I'm so glad you did. For good or bad, I've done it. I've achieved something I've wanted to do all my life.

Thank you to you, my readers, for reading my book. If you enjoyed it, please tell me. If you didn't, you now have the names of the people who told me to do it!

Ant Press Books

If you enjoyed this book, you may also enjoy these titles:

MEMOIR

Chickens, Mules and Two Old Fools by Victoria Twead (Wall Street Journal Top 10 bestseller)
Two Old Fools - Olé! by Victoria Twead
Two Old Fools on a Camel by Victoria Twead (New York Times bestseller x 3)
Two Old Fools in Spain Again by Victoria Twead
Two Old Fools in Turmoil by Victoria Twead
One Young Fool in Dorset by Victoria Twead
One Young Fool in South Africa by Joe & Victoria Twead
From Moulin Rouge to Gaudi's City by EJ Bauer
South to Barcelona: A New Life in Spain by Vernon Lacey
Don't Do It Like This: How NOT to move to Spain by Joe Cawley, Victoria Twead and Alan Parks
Fat Dogs and French Estates - Part I by Beth Haslam
Fat Dogs and French Estates - Part II by Beth Haslam
Fat Dogs and French Estates - Part III by Beth Haslam

Fat Dogs and French Estates - Part IV by Beth Haslam
Heartprints of Africa: A Family's Story of Faith, Love, Adventure, and Turmoil by Cinda Adams Brooks
Simon Ships Out: How One Brave, Stray Cat Became a Worldwide Hero by Jacky Donovan
Smoky: How a Tiny Yorkshire Terrier Became a World War II American Army Hero, Therapy Dog and Hollywood Star by Jacky Donovan
Smart as a Whip: A Madcap Journey of Laughter, Love, Disasters and Triumphs by Jacky Donovan
How not to be a Soldier: My Antics in the British Army by Lorna McCann
Cane Confessions: The Lighter Side to Mobility by Amy Bovaird
Completely Cats - Stories with Cattitude by Beth Haslam and Zoe Marr
Fresh Eggs and Dog Beds: Living the Dream in Rural Ireland by Nick Albert
Fresh Eggs and Dog Beds 2: Still Living the Dream in Rural Ireland by Nick Albert
Longing for Africa: Journeys Inspired by the Life of Jane Goodall. Part One: Ethiopia by Annie Schrank
One of its Legs are Both the Same by Mike Cavanagh
A Pocket Full of Days, Part 1 by Mike Cavanagh
Moment of Surrender: My Journey through Prescription Drug Addiction to Hope and Renewal by Pj Laube

FICTION

Parched by Andrew C Branham
A is for Abigail by Victoria Twead (Sixpenny Cross 1)
B is for Bella by Victoria Twead (Sixpenny Cross 2)
C is for the Captain by Victoria Twead (Sixpenny Cross 3)

NON-FICTION

How to Write a Bestselling Memoir by Victoria Twead

CHILDREN'S BOOKS

Seacat Simon: The Little Cat Who Became a Big Hero (age 8 to 11)
by Jacky Donovan
Morgan and the Martians by Victoria Twead

Ant Press Online

Why not check us out online? Follow Ant Press for news of forthcoming books and special publishing offers.

Website: www.antpress.org
Email: admin@antpress.org
Facebook: www.facebook.com/AntPress
Instagram: www.instagram.com/publishwithantpress
Twitter: www.twitter.com/Ant_Press

37361003R00122

Printed in Poland
by Amazon Fulfillment
Poland Sp. z o.o., Wrocław